The Great Game

The Great Game

The Coming Face Off
for Global Supremacy

By Dr. Kent Moors

MONEY MAP PRESS

www.moneymappress.com

Every morning, a gazelle wakes up.
It knows it must run faster than the fastest lion or it will be killed.
Every morning, a lion wakes up.
It knows it must outrun the slowest gazelle or it will starve to death.
It doesn't matter whether you are a lion or a gazelle.
When the sun comes up, you better start running.

This African proverb hung on my office wall for decades. It summarized a good deal of my professional life. The saying itself is of unknown origin, but has its own universe—appearing in thousands of locations on the Web, has its own sites, and is frequently used by supporters of everything from long-distance running to motivational speaking.

Contents

Acknowledgments

PUTTING THIS BOOK TOGETHER ushered in a tidal wave of memories, not all of them pleasant ones. My career has now spanned four and a half decades. That existence has owed so much to so many people. A number no longer still grace this earth, while others know we shared experiences that remain unspoken but never forgotten. I owe my life (quite literally) to some and my understanding to others. You don't walk through what I have experienced without having it leave an impression. When sitting down to write this, a question emerged. How do I honor those who have contributed to shaping who I am?

Perhaps the best way to acknowledge them is this.

I have learned a bit about what life means. The education has been interesting, painful, sobering, costly, rewarding, with some of it staying forever in that netherworld of still uncompleted events. But the same lesson was taught throughout.

If this life given to me by others has taught anything, it is this. You need to stand for something; you need to make other people's sacrifices—spouses, parents, family, friends, fellow countrymen—worth the effort.

It is the only way each of us can shoulder the legacy, the gift, the responsibility.

Especially these days. Conflict is a major part of what is experienced all around us. In fact, it has been the norm for some time. Peace seems to be the exception rather than the rule.

The Great Game has serious stakes.

I know about some of this personally. And that gives way to a ready emotion. I am writing these lines a few days before a very bittersweet anniversary.

It is one of two dates on which I should have died.

On both occasions, somebody else did instead. But what makes the upcoming anniversary more poignant is the victim. He was a fellow traveler in *The Great Game*, a close friend, and I put him there.

It was during a still classified operation that had gone very sour, compounded by the part of the world we were in. There was little in the way of a support structure to fall back on. I made a mistake that didn't help matters any and the op started unraveling.

What happened next is something that stays with me forever. He simply jumped into the line of fire and took a spray of bullets.

How do you "acknowledge" somebody for having done that? I couldn't later when I met with his widow and their two daughters back home. Can't do it now.

That I received two of my medals for the affair simply added to the irony and the pain. For his part, the man whose sacrifice let me keep on breathing received a star on a wall in northern Virginia. It does not even bear his name, given that the assignment is still classified.

He gave his life to save mine and even now his name cannot be mentioned.

I have never been able to shake the feeling of living on borrowed time. It is something that will be with me always. As one of my mentors used to say, "If you live long enough in this business you end up walking with ghosts."

Nobody told me at the time that some of those ghosts are more personal than others.

The conflict continues. Guiding you through this maze and providing some insight into how to provide greater financial security in the process, is how this book will help in navigating *The Great Game*.

However, there are also some folks I need to thank for bringing this work to print. They include David Sattler, Garrett Baldwin, Erica Bolton, Bob Keppel, and Jedd Canty. Each has provided significant help in various parts of the work and has contributed in countless other ways.

Publisher Mike Ward, Alex Williams, and the entire staff at *Money Map Press* have my continuing gratitude for putting together the most interesting and rewarding environment for ground-breaking work I have ever witnessed.

To Steve Christ, also at *Money Map*, I owe special thanks. This book simply would never have seen the light of day without his tireless efforts.

As with all things in my life, however, I thank most of all my wife Marina (and her fabled verbal whip that prods on the writer in me when I would prefer to do something else). My life would mean nothing without her.

The Great Game

1

The Great Game: War by Other Means

"THE BEST FORM OF DEFENSE IS ATTACK."
— KARL VON CLAUSEWITZ

♜

FROM THE OILFIELDS of Saudi Arabia, to mountain passes high in the Himalayas, to the very streets of London, peace is just an illusion.

Like a great chessboard that spans the globe, there is an economic war being fought on every front.

At the center of this "Great Game" are resources . . . oil, natural gas, strategic minerals and even water.

That's because the "easy-resource world" of the past no longer exists. Demand for these vital resources is skyrocketing while available supplies continue to shrink.

What we're now faced with is a geopolitical era of rivalry similar to the original Great Game of a century ago, but with new players and even higher stakes.

Back then, the game was much simpler. It was ruled by the age of empires. The Ottoman, Persian, Napoleonic, Russian, and British Empires dominated for over 150 years spanning the late 1700s to the early 1900s.

Like a great chessboard, the pieces they controlled were their armies, their natural resources, their economic strength, and their alliances. Empires rose and fell with every change on the board.

This long-enduring match only ended after two World Wars. From it, a new superpower was born. And in the decades that followed, America came to control the entire board.

But today, the U.S. is faced with some stiff competition—namely from China and Russia along with a lot of dangerous, secondary international players.

That includes India and Pakistan, who between them have 230 nuclear warheads and have already fought four wars since 1947. All of which means the stakes are infinitely higher than before.

But thanks to the overwhelming power of the U.S. military, true armed conflict as a Great Game strategy for the major powers is largely off the table. Attacking a far superior power is simply not a winning strategy.

And make no mistake, there's only one country in the world that can actually project power.

With 11 carrier groups and over 800 bases overseas, the U.S. military footprint spans the entire globe. As the only world-wide military

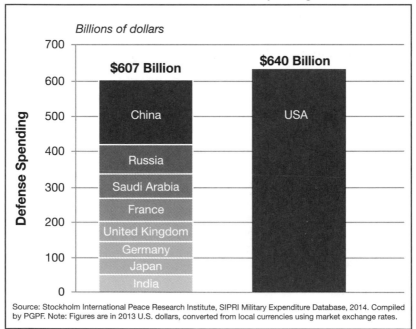

2014 Worldwide Defense Spending

Source: Stockholm International Peace Research Institute, SIPRI Military Expenditure Database, 2014. Compiled by PGPF. Note: Figures are in 2013 U.S. dollars, converted from local currencies using market exchange rates.

superpower, America's version of the colony is the military base, and no one's willing to play a game they can't win—at least not too far from its own borders.

At present, the U.S. spends more per year on defense than the next eight countries combined.

So while the United States has been happy to move its military chess pieces all about the globe, the rest of the world has decided not to play. In its wake, we're left with something that doesn't quite bend to the power of brute force.

Instead, it's a whole new ball game—one in which economics outweigh tanks, ships at sea, and airplanes. So while we don't have to worry about Russians pouring through the Fulda Gap anymore, today's battle lines have been drawn over natural resources, currency, trade, and economic strength.

It is war, but it is war by *other* means. And unlike the Great Game of the past, this struggle will be dominated largely by daring economic strokes.

That leaves the United States in unfamiliar territory.

With a fragile economy, staggering federal debt, unstable financial markets, and legitimate concerns with the dollar, the U.S. is now vulnerable in ways everyday Americans find difficult to understand.

AND WITH A deepening political divide between our leaders, we're entering a period that could be volatile for our economy—and for world economies as well.

This re-balancing of the economic power between nations could cause certain currencies to be destroyed—economies to weaken—companies to crumble. Even bedrocks of Wall Street could be at risk of bankruptcy.

In this new age of conflict, the Atlantic and Pacific Oceans simply will not act as some invisible wall that protects and insulates us from the outside world. And today, an upstart newcomer—otherwise known as China—has been playing the game to win, if not dominate.

That's why our own State Department now believes winning the battle for markets and resources is critical to our national security, global stability, and our entire foreign policy.

Take rare-earth elements, for instance.

Nobody had ever heard of bastnasite, cerium, lanthanum, praseodymium, neodymium, europium, or yttrium. That is, until China cornered the market.

Now, rare-earth elements have practically become household words. They're found in almost every 21st century product, including high-tech weapons systems, flat screen TVs, mobile phones, and computers.

These elements are so important that virtually no modern items can be produced without them, and China has been wielding them like a Shaolin Staff.

(By the way, that list also includes the same high-tech batteries that are supposed to be at the forefront of the green car revolution . . .)

Without rare earths, our 21st century economy would grind to halt . . . unless we agree to some shake down. Comrade Deng Xiaoping actually seemed to recognize this fact years earlier when he noted, "The Middle East has its oil, China has rare earth."

Since then, China has developed a monopoly on these elements, producing 97% of the world's current supply.

What's more, when they announced their plan for these elements looking forward to 2015, the Chinese said they would continue to reduce the export of these materials, and may actually stop some of them altogether.

That notion has sent the Pentagon into practical panic. As it turns out, our smart weapons aren't so smart without these Chinese exports.

"The Pentagon has been incredibly negligent," said Peter Leitner, a senior strategic trade adviser at the Defense Department from 1986 to 2007. "There are plenty of early warning signs that China will use its leverage over these materials as a weapon."

As it stands, the U.S. currently imports over $5 billion worth of these critical minerals and is almost completely dependent on foreign sources for 19 key specialty metals.

Supply shocks to any of them could unleash rampant inflation that would wind through every corner of our economy.

But that's just one small slice of the natural resources at play. The biggest prize is now—and will always be—access to steady supply of oil and natural gas.

Since the 1970s, Americans have been well aware of their vulnerability to these oil-based threats.

But with the emergence of dramatic new demand from places like China and India, even relatively small losses in supply can now send prices skyrocketing.

Combined with a sudden drop in the dollar, that could cost businesses billions, grinding our economic growth to halt.

The takeaway from all of this is simple: Today's Great Game is a battle of haves and have-nots with entire economies at stake.

If you *have* the resources, you can use them to your advantage. If you *don't* have them—you're going to see your influence in the world weakened in the future. All without firing a single shot.

Folks caught off guard by how this Great Game is going to evolve stand to lose as much as $1.41 trillion every year from Wall Street alone—and that's on the low end. In the bigger picture, there's over $20 trillion at stake.

That's why knowing who the players are and what's at stake is now more critical than ever.

This game essentially pits the U.S. and its allies and friends on one side of the board, and Russia and China and their allies and friends on the other.

Each is thinking five to ten moves ahead of everybody else on this chessboard, while the other players can only make one move at a time. Or react, out of desperation, when it's almost too late.

It's a struggle for dominance where the kings and queens of the game ultimately decide the strategy and actions of their "pieces."

In this case, countries like Britain, France, Japan, Iran, Saudi Arabia, Israel, Turkey, India, and others are merely middle-ranking pieces. They make for important allies, as long as they're willing to stick to the strategy.

As allies, countries like these are looking to their bigger "partners" to help them gain access to resources they otherwise wouldn't be able to secure for themselves. Or in some cases, they would like to get a kickback for simply helping out.

Every one of these players would like to have a larger share of the pie than the others, but above all, every one of them needs to get something as a matter of survival.

As for the pawns in this game, all of them are useful until they're not—in which case they become immediately expendable. In the end, it's a game about business. Pure and simple.

♜

BUT INSTEAD OF competing for actual control over geographic areas, pipelines, tanker routes, or petroleum consortiums, new technologies and big contracts are the prizes of the new Great Game.

Because if you can control the oil, gas, rare-earth metals, electricity, water, or even food, you have the ability to shape the destinies of all the other players. In this game, relative gains matter—but absolute gains are far more important.

In the end, it's a classic case of history repeating itself. But this time, it's a story about a scramble for resources.

Water in Pakistan and India . . . oil in South America . . . and believe it or not, figuring out ways to keep the lights on in London.

Nations are positioning their pieces on history's biggest geo-political chessboard to acquire the resources their countries need . . . by any means necessary.

And the outcome will determine who truly controls the balance of power in the future. From a geopolitical standpoint you're talking about a re-shuffling of the food chain from the top Superpowers right down to the bottom.

This is the Great Game.

And in this case, the winning strategy is to attack.

2

The Godfather of Geopolitics

"WHO RULES EASTERN EUROPE,
COMMANDS THE HEARTLAND;
WHO RULES THE HEARTLAND,
COMMANDS THE WORLD ISLAND;
WHO RULES THE WORLD ISLAND,
COMMANDS THE WORLD."
— SIR HALFORD MACKINDER

I T'S HARD TO LOOK at this battle for resources and not see the ghost of an obscure English academic, politician, and imperial explorer.

His name is Sir Halford Mackinder.

Born in 1861, Mackinder almost single-handedly invented both the academic study of geography and the concept of "geopolitics."

His rise began in 1904 with a major speech he gave at the Royal Geographical Society entitled *"The Geographical Pivot of History."* In it, Mackinder argued that the world had suddenly evolved into a "closed" system since the end of 19th century colonialism, which meant there was no more room for expansion.

According to Mackinder, the power politics of the future would be marked by a competition over the old territories rather than a quest for new ones.

The determining factor in this struggle would be geography. "Man and not nature initiates, but nature in large measure controls," wrote Mackinder.

Now for the first time, Mackinder posited, the geographical features of the world would define the nature of future struggles, the opposing sides, and the future areas of conflict.

Victory or defeat in this conflict Mackinder said, was now destined to hinge on the "pivot-state" delineated on the map below.

This "pivot state," or what he called "Eurasia," represented the world's most critical area, and whoever controlled this vast, landlocked region and its resources, Mackinder said, would effectively rule the globe.

Mackinder's Original Map Circa 1904

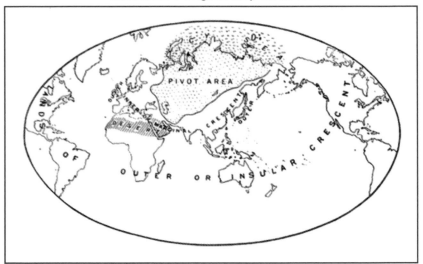

Later he renamed this area the "Heartland," which he described as "a great continuous patch in the north and center of the continent . . . from the icy, flat shore of Siberia to the torrid, steep coasts of Baluchistan and Persia."

Three things determined power in this region:

- Whoever ruled the Pivot would command the Heartland.
- Whoever ruled the Heartland would command the "World Island" (Europe, Russia and Asia)
- Whoever controlled the World Island would rule the world.

Ultimately, according to Mackinder, the state that controlled this Eurasian landmass would be able to organize its overwhelming human and material resources, to the detriment of the rest of the world.

Just outside the Heartland, he placed Germany, Austria, Turkey, India, China, the Middle East, Southeast Asia, and all of the lands immediately adjacent to the Pivot region in what he called the "Inner Crescent."

As for the insular nations of Britain, South Africa, Australia, the United States, Canada, and Japan, they each occupied a place in Mackinder's "Outer Crescent."

With it, the battle lines for much of 20th century conflict were formed.

Looking to the future, Mackinder contended that any state dominating the World Island would ultimately become the opponent of North America, and might use Eurasia's vast resources to overcome the Outer Crescent states.

Once this Eurasian power gained enough strength, victory would be all but inevitable.

Needless to say, Mackinder's map and the ideas behind it influenced generations of thinkers and politicians, from Karl Haushofer and Rudolph Hess to Henry Kissinger and Zbigniew Brzezinski.

It even undoubtedly influenced the work of a more famous British writer by the name of George Orwell.

And as Dr. Colin S. Gray, Professor of International Politics and Strategic Studies at the University of Reading, wrote:

> "By far the most influential geopolitical concept for Anglo-American statecraft has been the idea of a Eurasian 'heartland,' and then the complementary idea-as-policy of containing the heartland power of the day within, not to, Eurasia.
>
> From Harry S Truman to George Bush, the overarching vision of US national security was explicitly geopolitical and directly traceable to the heartland theory of Mackinder . . . Mackinder's relevance to the containment of a heartland-occupying Soviet Union in the cold war was so apparent as to approach the status of a cliché."

Over century after Mackinder's Heartland theory came into being, there's renewed interest from a resources standpoint in this area of the world.

In fact, the "Great Game" struggles of the twenty-first century are repeating the same historical patterns, but with China and its allies working to dominate as the Pivot Region or Heartland.

That includes a growing alliance with Russia, who occupies vast expanses of the Heartland and possesses vast human and natural resources, as well as thousands of nuclear weapons.

Viewed from a "Mackinderan" perspective, that pits the West against the East in the struggle to control the world's increasingly stretched resources.

This battleground includes familiar areas in Central Asia and the Caucuses where, with the help of Western investments, about 3.5% of the global oil supply is already produced and some 2.5% of the world's proven oil reserves are located. And while that might not sound like much, it's four times that of Norway and the UK combined.

It's also about 9.5% of all non-OPEC reserves and that's just the oil. At present, Central Asia is estimated to hold more than 11% of the world's proven gas reserves. These are mostly concentrated in Turkmenistan, which has lagged behind Kazakhstan and Azerbaijan in attracting outside investments. That means the opportunity for all the players here is tremendous.

This area stretches from the Caspian Sea in the west to China in the east and from Afghanistan in the south to Russia in the north. It is also sometimes referred to as Middle Asia.

This area has acted as a crossroads for people, goods, and ideas throughout history in what's historically recognized as the old Silk Road. For 1,500 years, these trade routes were the most enduring in human history.

Except these days the trade has less to do with silk, and everything to do with the flow of energy and economic interests.

In fact, just about every aspect of the escalating geopolitical tension in these areas has an energy element either directly or indirectly.

In broad terms, these Central Asian "battlegrounds" are largely dominated by players with a decidedly "home-field" advantage: China and Russia.

In this case, China's strategy is to use its financial clout to gain access to Central Asia's oil and natural gas.

Meanwhile, Russia's aims tend to be more political. Putin's goal is to maintain his dominance over Central Asian oil and gas exports in order to maintain his influence over the region and in Europe.

The Silk Road: The Crossroads for Over 1,500 Years

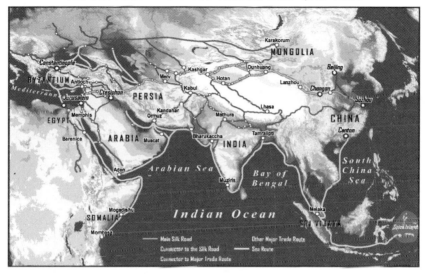

Given its landlocked geology that means establishing control over long haul pipelines in this region is critical.

That's why China has focused on pipeline development, including funding the construction of a pipeline system across Turkmenistan, Uzbekistan, and Kazakhstan to help supply its growing energy needs.

Now, Turkmenistan exports more gas to China than it sells to Russia's energy giant, Gazprom. The quantity is slated to go from 20 to 25 billion cubic meters (bcm) of gas in the near term and to reach 65 bcm by 2020. That's roughly equal to what Turkmenistan used to export via Russia.

As for America, its long-standing interest is to build alliances to promote the diversity of pipeline routes out of Central Asia, so that no single country can dominate the transit of oil and gas out of this "Pivot" region.

But like the old Silk Road, this story is full of twists, turns and dangers.

One of them has to do with nuclear weapons and the most precious resource of them all—water.

3

The Zero Line Crisis

"WE SHALL FIGHT A THOUSAND YEARS TO LIBERATE KASHMIR AND WE SHALL EAT GRASS, BUT WE WILL MAKE AN ATOMIC BOMB"
— ZULFIKAR ALI BHUTTO

♖

PAKISTAN HAS COME a long way since President Zulfikar Ali Bhutto committed to acquiring nuclear weapons in the wake of his country's devastating defeat to India in the 1971 Bangladesh war.

Forty-two years later, his country is now armed to the teeth with them, and the economy is a mess.

As for the dispute over Kashmir, it could boil over at any moment leading to the world's first regional nuclear war.

That's why it's critical that Americans understand exactly what's at stake. With roughly 230 nuclear warheads between them, India and Pakistan are literally gambling with the fate of the rest of the world.

In fact, according to a recent study, a nuclear war between India and Pakistan would set off a global famine that could kill two billion people and effectively end human civilization.

Even if this conflict was limited in scope, a nuclear exchange between the two would wreak havoc in the atmosphere and devastate crop yields. Those effects would be multiplied as global food markets went deeper into turmoil.

Scientists warn such a clash would also cause climate changes which would destroy crops and cause more than a billion people to starve.

As it developed, radiation clouds would contaminate farmland, while soot in the atmosphere would wipe out crops with cooler temperatures and reduced rainfall.

"Even these smaller arsenals pose an existential threat to our civilization, if not to our species. It would certainly end modern society as we know it," according to author Dr. Ira Helfand.

Specifically, the study noted, a nuclear war in South Asia would release black carbon aerosol particles that would cut U.S. corn and soybean production by 10% over a decade.

Those particles would also reduce Chinese rice production by an average of 21% over a four-year period and by another 10% over the subsequent six years. Even more devastating, China's wheat crop would drop by 50% in just the first year after the hypothetical Indo-Pak nuclear war.

And if something isn't done quickly, the world may find itself staring at the very real possibility of this scenario erupting over what I call: **"The Zero Line."**

This is one of the most important—if not THE most important story—happening in the world right now. In fact, recent public statements from both sides suggest they already have their fingers on the nuclear triggers.

Warnings have even begun to appear in Indian newspapers that a nuclear war is not only a very real possibility, but could be potentially imminent.

These notices provided vivid details on the "do's" and "don'ts," including the construction of bunkers, which should be stocked with "non-perishable foods and water" and toilet facilities and the storage of "ample candles and battery lights."

Jammu and Kashmir Police's Civil Defense and State Disaster Response released this advisory in the wake of several Zero Line "incidents," detailing the steps people should take in the event of a nuclear war.

"Expect some initial disorientation as the blast wave may blow down and carry away many prominent and familiar features," the notice advised.

The notice came barely two weeks after skirmishes between Indian and Pakistani soldiers along the de facto border killed five soldiers, three of them Pakistani.

And you will likely find this next excerpt even more alarming.

"Stay down after the initial shock wave, wait for the winds to die down and debris to stop falling," the notice advises. "If blast wave does not arrive within five seconds of the flash you were far enough from the ground zero and initial radiation exposure will not exceed 150 rads."

Keep in mind that these dire messages are not coming from an over-zealous politician, looking to make a name for himself. These warnings were posted by *India's Disaster Response Force.*

Now when I say Zero Line, I'm referring to the border that runs between India and Pakistan in Kashmir. This border is also known as "The Line of Control." But, in reality, there is no control over either the Zero Line or Kashmir.

Since the partition of British India in 1947, Kashmir has become a hotly contested territory claimed by both India and Pakistan, turning them into bitter arch rivals.

♜

THIS ANIMOSITY HAS its roots in both religion and historical developments, and is epitomized by the long-running conflict over the state of Jammu and Kashmir

India claims the entire state of Jammu and Kashmir, and as of 2010, administers approximately 43% of the region, including most of Jammu, the Kashmir Valley, Ladakh, and the Siachen Glacier. However, India's claims are contested by Pakistan, which controls approximately 37% of Kashmir, namely Azad Kashmir and the northern areas of Gilgit Baltistan.

Over 60 years after the British partition, Pakistanis still believe that Jammu and Kashmir should have become part of Pakistan because the majority of the state's population, concentrated in the valley of Kashmir, is Muslim.

In fact, Pakistan's very name is derived from: P for Punjab, A for the Afghanis of the north-west frontier, K for Kashmir, S for Sind and Tan denoting Baluchistan.

The attempts to resolve this dispute through political discussions have been unsuccessful, resulting in simmering tensions and a never-ending series of skirmishes and outright wars.

The Most Hotly Contested Real Estate in the World

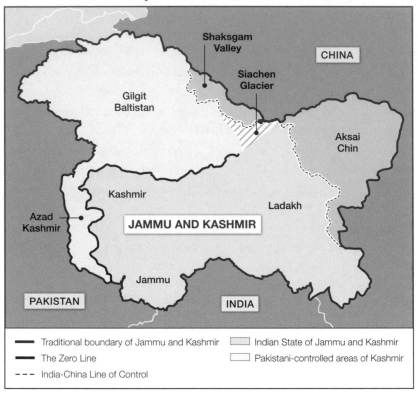

Shaksgam
Valley

CHINA

Siachen
Glacier

Gilgit
Baltistan

Aksai
Chin

Kashmir

Ladakh

Azad
Kashmir

JAMMU AND KASHMIR

Jammu

PAKISTAN

INDIA

—— Traditional boundary of Jammu and Kashmir   ▭ Indian State of Jammu and Kashmir

—— The Zero Line   ▭ Pakistani-controlled areas of Kashmir

--- India-China Line of Control

In fact, India and Pakistan have fought at least three wars over Kashmir, including the Indo-Pakistani Wars of 1947, 1965, and 1999.

In 1972, under the terms of the Simla agreement, the ceasefire line was later renamed the Line of Control (LoC). Today, this Zero Line is the most dangerous, militarized border on the planet.

Sometimes referred to as "Asia's Berlin Wall," the Zero Line runs about 460 miles long. On the Indian-controlled side, about 150 yards inside the border, India has constructed 340 miles of double row 12-foot-high, razor sharp, electrified barb wired fencing.

The fencing is equipped with motion sensors, infrared imaging devices, lighting systems and alarms, all of which act as "fast alert signals" to keep out Pakistani infiltrators.

Where the fencing stops, row after row after row of landmines begin. There are thousands of them buried just under the surface.

And, on both sides of The Zero Line, the Indian and Pakistani armies have deployed an estimated 650,000 troops, along with tens of thousands of police and paramilitary forces.

On a nearly daily basis, this already fragile cease-fire between India and Pakistan is violated, as automatic and small-arms fire, RPGs, rockets and mortars are exchanged. All told, over 47,000 people have lost their lives during this so-called "cease fire."

They've even taken this bloody conflict high into the mountains. At 20,000 feet above sea level, the Siachen Glacier along the Zero Line has been nicknamed "the highest battleground on earth."

The World's Highest Battlefield

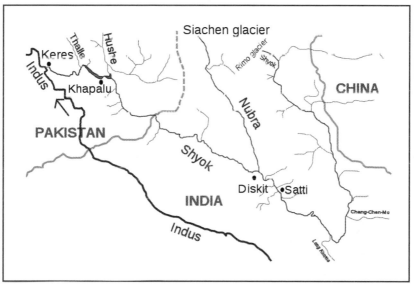

It's a place where temperatures can plummet to 70 degrees below zero and winds of up to 100 mph can come up without warning.

This frozen landscape houses 150 manned posts and 6,000 troops from the Pakistani and Indian militaries.

And they're ready to wage war as soon as the orders come in since both sides of the Zero Line conflict follow a strict doctrine of "shoot first . . . and never ask questions."

India and Pakistan have been in almost constant conflict over this area since the 1972 Simla Agreement failed to clearly spell out who controlled the glacier. It began in earnest on April 13, 1984, when India launched "Operation Meghoot" and gained almost complete control of the glacier.

In an historical quirk, the entire operation was set into motion only after India's Arctic gear supplier in London tipped them off about recent purchases by Islamabad. According to a now-retired Pakistani army colonel, "Once the Indians got wind of it, they ordered 300 outfits—twice as many as we had—and rushed their men up to Siachen."

When the Pakistanis arrived, they found a 300-man Indian battalion dug into the highest mountaintops.

Today, the blood continues to be spilled in these high mountain passes, with reported incidents of firing logged almost every week.

"What surprises us," says an Indian army officer in Srinagar, "is that the happenings in Siachen just do not seem to be affected by anything that happens at the diplomatic level."

More than 2,000 people have died in this inhospitable terrain, mostly due to weather extremes and the natural hazards of mountain warfare. It has given rise to a famous local saying, "The land is so barren and the passes so high that only the best of friends and fiercest of enemies come by."

But as bad as the current state of affairs is between India and Pakistan, it could soon get a lot worse. Pakistani Prime Minister, Nawaz Sharif recently warned that Kashmir—home the Zero Line—is about to boil over.

"Kashmir is a flashpoint," said Sharif in a December 2013 statement, "and can trigger a fourth war between the two nuclear powers at any time."

The Prime Minister went on to say that he had a dream of seeing held-Kashmir free from the Indian occupation and hoped that this dream could turn into reality during his lifetime.

Asked about Sharif's "threat", Indian Prime Minister Manmohan Singh told reporters, "There is no scope of Pakistan winning any such war in my lifetime."

Now is that posturing? Absolutely. But it doesn't diminish the seriousness of the threat. Privately, the U.S. government is concerned that the next conflict could put billions of people in jeopardy. Yet, Americans aren't hearing a single word about this on the news—or from Washington D.C.

Making matters exponentially worse is this: Much of the military in Pakistan is under the control of radical, Islamic factions. At least eight radical Islamic groups—including Al-Qaeda and the Taliban—hold sway there.

It's no coincidence that Osama Bin Laden was shielded for years from the U.S.—not far from Islamabad. He was found holed up next to the Pakistani equivalent of our own West Point.

Then there's Hamid Gul a.k.a. the "Father" of the Taliban. Besides being a Pakistani General, he was also the Director General of Inter-Services Intelligence, Pakistan's chief spy agency. He even once led a dangerous military insurgency across the Zero Line.

Today, these extreme groups tied to the Pakistani military view this as a Holy War. So much so they've all teamed up—and formed a coalition called the United Jihad Council (UJC). The UJC was created to unify and focus efforts of various armed militant groups fighting against the Indian rule in Kashmir.

Also known as the Muttahida Jihad Council, the group is currently headed by Syed Salahuddin, the leader of the Hizb-ul-Mujahideen (meaning party of holy warriors), the largest Jihad group operating in the Indian administered part of Jammu and Kashmir.

In a June 2012 interview, Salahuddin declared his intention to start attacking Pakistan if Pakistan stopped backing his jihadis in Jammu and Kashmir.

"We are fighting Pakistan's war in Kashmir," Salahuddin said, "and if it withdraws its support, the war would be fought inside Pakistan."

So Pakistan's reputation as an unstable and violent country located at the epicenter of global jihadism is well earned. Unfortunately, it's the only Muslim-majority state out of the 50 or so in the world to have successfully developed nuclear weapons.

It's perfectly sensible to believe that Pakistan might not exactly be the safest place on Earth to warehouse nuclear weapons let alone continue to pursue them.

This arms race between heated rivals escalated dramatically in the 1990s and has been accelerating ever since.

In May 1998, India conducted underground nuclear tests in the western desert state of Rajasthan near the border with Pakistan. In response, Pakistan conducted six tests in Baluchistan.

In the same year, Pakistan tested its longest range missile, the 1,500 km (932 mile) Ghauri missile, named after a 12th century Muslim warrior who conquered part of India.

Today, Pakistan is a nation with 120 nuclear warheads under its control, while India controls 110. So the math alone is this area is very simple and very dangerous.

If 100 nuclear warheads goes off, it's game over for everybody—everybody in India—everybody in Pakistan—essentially everybody on the planet.

That's why it is so critical to our entire foreign policy—not to mention the policies of other countries.

♖

NOW ADMITTEDLY, WE'VE had own our share of close calls, threats, and posturing over the years. The Cuban Missile Crisis in the '60s was as close as they come.

But during the Cold War, we all became familiar with the term "MAD"—or "Mutually Assured Destruction." It's what kept the U.S. and the USSR from firing nuclear weapons at each other. Because it didn't matter who fired first—both sides would lose in the end.

However, the situation today is quite different, which is why a lot of people in world governments—governments I advise, their militaries, and intelligence agencies—are keeping a close eye on and developing action plans around this ongoing conflict.

Here's why . . . "MAD" may not be enough to stop the Zero Line crisis from boiling over.

Mutually assured destruction is not necessarily a big concern of the Taliban and other Islamic radicals, who still hold a great deal of influence over many parts of the Pakistani military. And remember, the government and the military don't always see eye-to-eye in that country.

On top of that, Lt. Gen. Khalid Kidwai stepped down in December 2013 as the head of the Strategic Plans Division (SPD), the entity in charge of Pakistan's nuclear weapons. Established in 2000, Kidwai has been the only face the SPD has ever known.

International security experts have long revered him for his leadership. In the words of South Asia security specialist Michael Krepon, "his competence inspires the view that he is indispensable."

Keep in mind this is a country where nuclear weapons are reportedly moved by delivery van and travel on dangerous and congested roads. That includes small tactical nukes—which have received great interest within the Pakistani military.

Add it all up, and it's not hard to see why this area of the world is so dangerous.

That may be why President Clinton once remarked, "The most dangerous place you could argue in the world today is the Indian subcontinent and the line of control in Kashmir."

From my dealings in the area, I can tell you President Clinton was absolutely, positively correct in his assessment.

After all, when it comes to a nuclear war with India, the Pakistani government has mandated a trigger happy, "First Use" policy. And you can probably figure out what a "First Use" policy means.

But what you really need to understand is the "trigger event" that can collapse this house of cards, because in Pakistan's eyes it has already been "triggered."

That's not my conclusion either. It's the conclusion of 20 separate UN panels. Unfortunately, those findings were also confirmed by India's official counter-terrorism expert Ajai Sahni when he issued this warning.

Regarding a nuclear war with Pakistan, he said, "Everyone seems to think it's a question of when, not whether."

Now, if this scares you—it should. Because here's what many in my circle—meaning world governments and intelligence agencies—fear could set everything into motion.

The truth is Pakistan can initiate its "First Use" policy regarding nuclear war with India at any moment . . . over water. Specifically, over three contested rivers.

This tripwire began in 1960, when Pakistan and India sat down to negotiate a tense agreement called the Indus Waters Treaty. This treaty was beyond critical since it delineated the rules for how to handle six major rivers that supply *both* nations with fresh water.

According to the agreement, India was to receive control over the three "eastern" rivers: The Beas, Ravi and Sutlej. Meanwhile, Pakistan received control over the Chenab, the Jhelum, and the Indus River.

These three rivers provide Pakistan with:

- **90% of its freshwater for agriculture.**
- **50% of the country's employment.**
- **And 25% of its GDP.**

The Rivers of Life

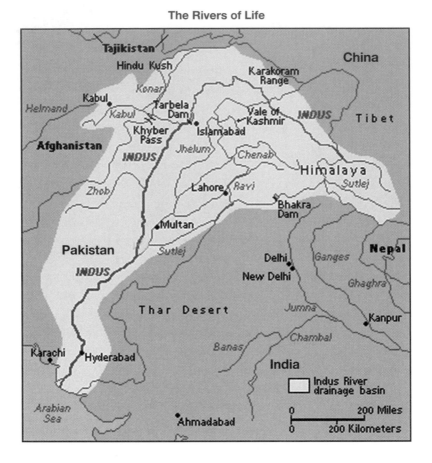

So, it's no wonder Pakistanis call these rivers "the water of life."

Unfortunately, it's also no wonder they're the source of this Zero Line crisis because Pakistan has accused India of stealing them. The accusation stems from a clause in the Indus Waters Treaty. One it appears nobody in Pakistan cared to read in 1960.

That's because the Chenab, Jhelum, and Indus Rivers all originate in India before flowing into Pakistan. And a clause in the treaty gives India the right to use these rivers for:

- Transport
- Power generation
- Irrigation

Transport isn't the red flag here. But the other two, power generation and irrigation, are.

Thanks to this treaty, India has free range to use these rivers for their own needs, before the water ever crosses the Zero Line between the two countries.

Take a look at this chart. You'll see—clear as day—why this is such a big problem.

In 1960, when Pakistan signed the Indus Waters Treaty, they had a population of 45 million people. Today, they have 201 Million.

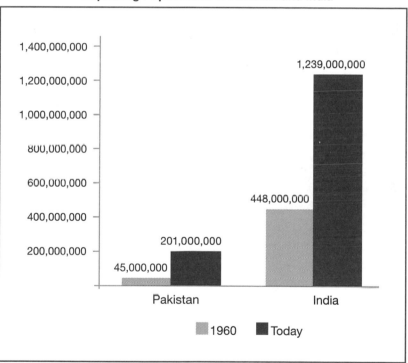

Exploding Populations in Pakistan and India

And when India signed the treaty, they had a population of 448 million people. Today, they have 1.2 billion.

This part of the crisis is simple: More people equal more electricity. Since 1980, India's electricity demands have shot up over 613%, while folks there have seen their electricity prices spike 500%.

And if this wasn't bad enough, India has to double their energy production capabilities within the next few years just to satisfy their growing population.

In July 2012, one of the world's worst blackouts left more than 700 million people in India without power, leading to fears that protests and even riots would erupt. These blackouts raised serious concerns about India's ability to meet the nation's increasing appetite for energy as it aspires to become an economic superpower.

Twenty of India's 28 states were hit by power cuts, along with the capital, New Delhi.

Experts agree India must invest heavily in its power infrastructure to meet the needs of its 1.2 billion people—and to keep up with China, its only serious rival as a future global superpower besides the U.S.

So they're faced with few choices. And the choice they initially made is a dangerous one.

In 2013, they began a bold plan to boost their hydropower capabilities by 4,000%. And they have targeted the Zero Line rivers that flow into Pakistan to accomplish this.

India is now planning for at least 45 hydropower facilities on the rivers granted to Pakistan in the Indus Waters Treaty. So essentially, they're planning to dam off much of the flow of these rivers before they cross the Zero Line.

But there's more to this story. Besides choking the flow of water into Pakistan for energy purposes, India is also tapping into Pakistan's rivers for irrigation, because the Indus Waters Treaty allows for it.

South Asia already has the highest number of food-insecure people with 300 million undernourished, and India accounts for 250 million of them. Producing enough food to feed its own people has long been a top priority.

This has created a line in the sand moment in Islamabad.

You see, at any given time, India only has enough water reserves to satisfy its nation's needs for 120 days.

So they aren't left with much of a safety net if they experience a severe drought, or a disruption in water distribution. What's more, the groundwater supplies for Delhi, Mumbai, Hyderabad and Chennai are declining so fast, it's estimated they'll be gone in a few years.

So they can't tap into their own water to boost their irrigation needs.

But in the bigger scheme of things, tapping into Pakistan's is an even more dangerous gamble because they're already dry to the bone.

While India has 120 days of water, Pakistan only has enough water reserves for 30 days.

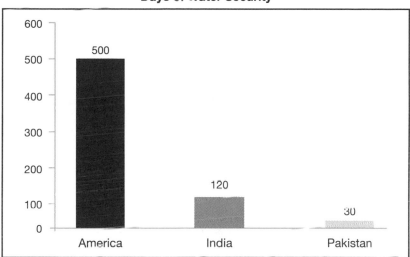

Days of Water Security

This situation has gotten so severe; Pakistanis are stealing water from public pipes and selling it out of the back of trucks in the slums of Karachi. According to reports, this water market has become a $500 million a year business.

So we're quickly reaching the point of war over the most essential resource of them all . . . water.

In fact, in 2008, India suffered a horrific attack in Mumbai over water that was carried out by Pakistani extremists. One of the alleged ringleaders, Hafiz Sayeed, justified the atrocity by accusing India of committing "water terrorism" against Pakistan.

As startling as that incident was, its radius of destruction was limited. That doesn't change the fact that water scarcity will transform Pakistan into a totally failed state within a decade.

What you are left with is a dangerous equation many fear will lead to one conclusion: a massive conflict. Of course, as you can see, this Zero Line crisis is about a lot more than just disputed territory.

It's also a story about a resource war. Two resources in particular—water and energy.

But I believe there is a silver lining to be found here. At the moment, India and Pakistan are doing a lot of posturing—or face-saving. Neither side wants to start a nuclear war, but neither wants to be seen as the weaker side, either.

So imagine this through the view of this Great Game—look at it like a game of chess—India and Pakistan are essentially at a stalemate.

They've tried moving their pieces to get the other side to back down, but it's not happening. So essentially, neither side has a winning move without having to make a major sacrifice.

However, given the threat of extreme Islamic elements, where MAD isn't necessarily a deterrent, nobody wants to take a chance this situation could become unhinged.

So what's happening are some of the major international players are getting involved in this Zero Line Crisis. And that's exactly what India and Pakistan need. Better yet, they want help. And this is good news.

In fact, there are two very big solutions in play right now—and I believe they can stop this Zero Line Crisis from escalating into a nuclear war crisis. One is a solution for the water crisis—and one for the energy tensions.

And they are both being driven by players outside of India and Pakistan.

4

Peace, War, and Intrigue Along the New Silk Road

A LONG THE NEW Silk Road, which carries the fruits of modern-day trade between China and Europe, energy and water are both hotly contested battlegrounds in the Great Game.

One of these battlegrounds revolves around the Indus River, a key hotspot between India and Pakistan that could one day lead to the unthinkable.

That's because both countries depend on the river and its tributaries for agricultural and drinking water. Now, disagreements over this critical water have brought this long-simmering conflict to a head.

And I don't have to remind you what's at stake. Pakistan has aimed some of its 120 nuclear warheads towards India, while India has pointed some of its 110 nuclear warheads right back.

The question now is how this brewing conflict can be resolved short of war. But thanks to a new technology, there are now hopes that this brewing water crisis won't lead to nuclear war.

The solution to this crisis just may be desalination.

Desalination is the process of removing salt from seawater. It's an ancient process that makes salt water useable and drinkable. Mankind has captured evaporated seawater, leaving the salt behind, or distilled that water to remove the salt, for centuries. What's more, ocean-going ships use this process today to supply water to their passengers during long voyages.

With 99% of the earth's water being saltwater, India, Pakistan and many other countries in the world, especially those with long coastlines, will someday likely have to turn to desalination to supply their water.

In fact, India and Pakistan are already working toward that goal.

India's water desalination business is predicted to triple to $1.2 billion by 2017, with 500 plants in operation. Meanwhile, Pakistan's efforts are much less evolved, but the country does have 12 operating desalination plants and is constructing a massive new plant in Karachi.

The stumbling block has been cost. Conventional desalination processes, such as reverse osmosis, multi-stage flash distillation, membrane distillation and others are expensive. The cost is five times greater than extracting and purifying water from rivers, lakes or groundwater.

But a new technology, from a defense contractor better known for the A-10 Thunderbolt II, the F-35 fighter plane, the Joint Light Tactical Vehicle, and the Hellfire II missile, could slash the amount of energy needed to remove salt from seawater, drastically reducing its cost.

Developed by Lockheed Martin, the process uses a microscopically thin carbon wafer of graphene to convert saltwater to freshwater 100 times faster than conventional techniques, while also cutting energy costs by 99%.

Lockheed originally began developing graphene for use in their core businesses, including aircraft and spacecraft. They discovered that this new material had the potential to become the most efficient water filter of all time almost by accident.

Conventional reverse osmosis pushes saltwater at high pressure through thick membranes that allow the water to pass through but trap the salt. This process requires a lot of energy and time.

But because graphene is only one atom thick—the thinnest material on the planet—saltwater can now be pushed through holes about one nanometer, or one-billionth of a meter, with very little energy. The graphene is so thin it can even remove radioactive material from water. It also, for reasons scientists don't fully understand, allows water through and almost nothing else.

This "miracle material" is as flexible as rubber, 300 times stronger than steel, and has the potential to be a game-changer in the desalination industry.

The material does present some challenges, but Lockheed scientists say that ultimately, graphene filters could be easily retrofitted to existing desalination plants, making them far more efficient and less costly to operate. In fact, Lockheed is currently marketing the filter under the name Perforene™, and is seeking partners to help commercialize it.

The commercial potential, as well as the political ramifications, are huge.

India is now allocating $92.1 billion a year towards solving its water crisis. Meanwhile, Pakistan has committed $300 billion towards water technology.

Needless to say, the new technology could have major geopolitical implications.

Global water shortages pose huge threats of terror and war, according to intelligence experts around the world. Millions of people die each year from water-related diseases, while millions more lack access to clean water.

But with this new technology, desalination now becomes economically viable in even the poorest countries providing clean drinking water to the 780 million people who can't access it now.

And in the bigger picture, this new technology now means the U.S. appears to have made a major move in the Great Game, easing tensions in the region by helping provide abundant, safe water with a fraction of the energy of conventional technology.

♜

BUT BETTER DESALINATION technology is not the only bright spot in this dangerous hot spot.

There's another move afoot that promises to stabilize the situation between India and Pakistan and reshuffle the deck for the major players. That factor is energy.

Or, more specifically, the logistics of moving energy resources from the wells where it's produced to the homes, businesses, and other facilities that need it.

You see, along the Silk Road, where Asian traders brought their wares and culture to Europe centuries ago, there's a "New Silk Road" forming.

Once a 4,000-mile route used by Chinese silk traders beginning in the Han Dynasty, this New Silk Road is transforming the development of the Indian subcontinent, the Middle East, and Europe as profoundly as the original Silk Road did centuries ago.

Of course, these roads are well worn. It was once the path trod by Venetian trader Marco Polo, whose actions fueled a Western appetite for the treasures of the east, such as tea, silk, gunpowder, and porcelain. Camel caravans and ships that travelled those routes brought not only goods and services, but new ideas from Asia to Europe and back.

But this time the coin of the realm isn't silk, household goods, cultural differences or political and religious ideas.

On this go-round, the currency is energy, particularly natural gas.

And one of its major pieces is the Trans-Afghanistan Pipeline, also known as the Turkmenistan-Afghanistan-Pakistan-India pipeline, or TAPI. This proposed 1,700-kilometer pipeline is designed to run through the heart of a major strategic portion of the Great Game, bringing much needed energy supplies from Turkmenistan into India, Pakistan, and China.

As designed, this pipeline is of tremendous political and economic importance to both Pakistan and India. In fact, for those reasons, it's often referred to as the "Peace Pipeline."

♜

BUT UNLIKE THE Indus River, no treaty or agreement governs the use, ownership or management of TAPI. Every country along its proposed route, as well as the U.S. and the Asian and European countries that will depend on it, has a different opinion on who should construct and manage it, as well as how it should be run.

As it unfolds the region's former Soviet republics and Indian subcontinent nations find themselves in a very strategic position. It's one that could change the energy flow along with the markets between Asia, the Middle East, and Europe.

The Peace Pipeline

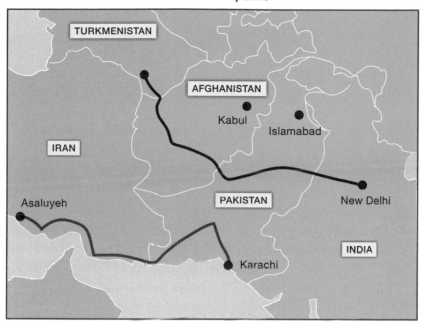

Projected to cost $7.6 billion, the TAPI pipeline will begin in a Turkmenistan gas field that could possess more than $8.2 trillion worth of energy, making it potentially the second largest natural gas field in the world.

It will transport gas from Turkmenistan, one of the Turkic states in Central Asia, and ultimately double the amount of Turkmen gas exports to China. In fact, China recently signed $100 billion in agreements to create energy-driven strategic alliances in the Turkmenistan region.

A portion of this region in Turkmenistan has been dubbed the "black sand" desert. It has only one person every 2.5 miles and rains once a decade, but it contains one of the world's largest reserves of oil and gas.

For China, which views energy in geopolitical as well as economic terms, the importance of the TAPI pipeline follows a long string of energy projects in the region.

Turkmenistan is already China's largest foreign supplier of natural gas, accounting for over half of the Asian giant's gas imports, or 21.3 billion cubic meters (bcm) as of 2012.

Prior to the proposed TAPI pipeline, the two countries developed the first natural gas production facility at Bagtyyarlyk in 2009, when they also opened the first pipeline carrying Turkmen gas to the east.

And more recently, a new Chinese-built $600 million facility was launched in Turkmenistan, further tying China's energy future to the country, bringing China's total investment in Turkmenistan's natural gas industry to $4 billion.

Gas from the new plant will flow through the 1,833-kilometer Turkmenistan-Uzbekistan-Kazakhstan-China pipeline, which also has significant geopolitical consequences in itself. Formerly, China depended upon Russian export routes for its gas from the region.

But the Chinese didn't stop there. Turkmenistan President Gurbanguly Berdymukhamedov, is planning a second processing plant at Galkynysh. That will add another 30 bcm annually to Turkmenistan's production capacity. By 2020, the country plans to export 65 bcm to China.

Much of that newly available gas will travel along a new, yet-to-be-built line across Uzbekistan, Tajikistan, and Kyrgyzstan, which has been dubbed Line D. Although those three countries are not allowed to tap the pipeline to supply their own energy needs, China has promised significant fees to them, with $1 billion annual payments to Kyrgyzstan alone.

For China, these projects along with the TAPI form the centerpiece in its Great Game strategy. In fact, Chinese President Xi Jinping has repeatedly called for a new "Silk Road economic belt." That maneuver, the Chinese say, would further link them with their overland neighbors, and include trade agreements, joint infrastructure projects, and other economic ties. Extending its influence even further, China has already inked deals with Romania, Serbia and Hungary.

As a corollary to that initiative, China has also proposed a "maritime Silk Road" to promote economic, security, and infrastructure projects and initiatives between China and its Asia-Pacific neighbors. Beijing has also strengthened its ties with Pakistan, building overland and undersea tunnels, a new rail link, and cooperating on other infrastructure and trade projects.

But there are significant challenges for the TAPI beyond the expected financial and technological considerations. The TAPI pipeline's planned route runs through the Taliban heartland of Kandahar in south Afghanistan, then through the volatile Pakistani city of Quetta, and the fringes of the Balochistan badlands. There, separatists are staging an insurgency against government forces, and both the governments in Kabul and Islamabad appear to have little control over the area.

But the Chinese aren't the only major geopolitical power in this part of the Great Game.

Because the pipeline will wind through the Kandahar province of Afghanistan, it will help eliminate Afghanistan's dependency on Iranian oil, just as the Chinese are increasing their oil imports from Iran. Iran is already China's second largest source of imported oil.

That will cripple Iran's economy, while simultaneously weakening Russian influence in the region. Even Russia's natural gas giant, Gazprom, recently stopped buying Turkmen gas.

And the catalyst for Afghanistan's involvement in the New Silk Road? It's the country currently pulling its troops out of the country: the United States. In fact, the TAPI pipeline would be big geopolitical win for the U.S.

America formulated its own New Silk Road initiative for Afghanistan in 2011. Its goal was to help the country resume traditional trading routes and activities and reconstruct the infrastructure that had been destroyed by decades of conflict.

A component of this Afghanistan initiative involves China, since recent Sino-American meetings have focused on the role China could play following the U.S. withdrawal. So it's possible that an uneasy détente between the world's two greatest powers, the U.S. and China, could rule the region, at least for the foreseeable future.

Both the U.S. and China are interested in the region for the same reasons. Meanwhile, the Chinese have had recent conflicts with the East Turkestan Islamic Movement (Etim), a militant Uighur group linked to the Taliban and Pakistani jihadi networks. So it's in their best interest to pacify this dangerous area of the world as well. The TAPI is just part of the solution.

Both China and the U.S. may realize that working together to control the region and extract its rich natural resources is preferable to sustaining military conflicts in Afghanistan, long known as "the graveyard of empires."

Working together, the two adversaries could also go a long way toward defusing the situation in India and Pakistan as well. As a major new supply of energy for both countries, the TAPI pipeline promises to be a key step forward in that area.

But in the Great Game, alliances can disappear as quickly as oil poured onto desert sand, and agreements forged with unstable governments or terrorist organizations can change overnight.

And as you'll see, China has 1.3 billion reasons behind every move it makes.

5

The Dragon in the Room

"LET CHINA SLEEP, FOR WHEN SHE AWAKES,
SHE WILL SHAKE THE WORLD."

— NAPOLEON

♖

WHETHER YOU REALIZE it or not, there's only one setting on the Chinese throttle: It's full steam ahead.

As one of the Great Game's biggest and most dangerous players, China has come a long way since it began to introduce major economic reforms beginning in 1978.

At the time, China was one of the poorest countries in the world. Today, this young upstart is getting close to leaving Uncle Sam and the rest of the Western world in its wake.

As a Great Game competitor, the Chinese are playing for keeps and they're taking no prisoners.

In fact, according to the International Monetary Fund (IMF), China—not the U.S.—has the largest economy in the world.

That happened a full five years ahead of schedule.

Meaning that America's run at the top of the economic heap is over. The U.S. has been the global leader since overtaking the British Empire in 1872.

The data used in the calculation comes from the 2011 International Comparison Program (ICP), which calculates GDP statistics by factoring in purchasing-power parity (PPP)—a measure of what money can actually buy in different economies.

These statistics show that China's economy is far larger than previously thought. Its GDP was actually $13.5 trillion in 2011, compared with the $7.3 trillion calculated using exchange rates.

That means China was in striking distance of the United States' $15.5 trillion economy back in 2011.

The U.S. Loses Its Spot at the Top

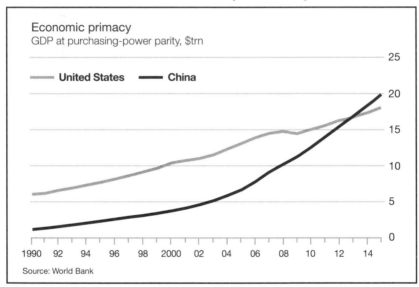

According to Dr. John J. Mearsheimer, "If the Chinese economy continues growing at a brisk clip in the next few decades, the United States will once again face a potential peer competitor, and great-power politics will return in full force. . . But if those who are bullish on China are correct, it will almost certainly be the most important geopolitical development of the twenty-first century, for China will be transformed into an enormously powerful country."

Simply put, the pace and scale of China's economic transformation have no historical precedent.

And even after all these years of double-digit growth, China's 1.3 billion people are hungry for even more. No matter how much the Chinese put on their collective plate, it's never enough.

For starters, just take a look at this picture . . .

"It looks like just another beautiful day in Paris. But what is it really?"

With the Eiffel Tower in the background, you would assume you're looking at a picture taken in France. But you would be wrong. It's actually a scene in Tianducheng, China.

Tianducheng was built by the Chinese to be a near replica of Paris. It's fit with an Eiffel tower, beautiful architecture and fabulous avenues. There's everything you would expect to be in Paris. But look closely—there's no one there.

It has come to be known as a "Ghost City." With a 2% occupancy rate, China's "Ghost City Paris" is 98% empty. And while the original Paris was built over 2,260 years ago, construction on China's Paris began in 2007.

And it's not the only Ghost City the Chinese have built. They've also built the Hennan Province Ghost City. In it, there are empty skyscrapers and buildings as far as the eye can see. That's because the Hennan Province Ghost City was built for 5 million people—but no one lives there either.

Then there is Chenggong—another Chinese Ghost City. There are rows of apartment complexes built to house 100,000 people. And yet there's not one single occupant. There are even two universities in this Ghost City, but there's not a single student who attends class.

And in the Kangbashi District, there is the City of Ordos, nick-named *"the Dubai of China."* It has everything, like beautiful museums and a majestic theatre complex. But no one's around to visit them, because even though it has enough housing for 1.5 million people, China's Dubai is nearly empty. Its population is believed to be around 28,000 people, or just 1/75th of the real Dubai.

There's a replica of Manhattan's financial district being built right now in another Chinese Ghost City, Tianjin. It's a replica of Wall Street, and it'll be empty when it's done.

In total, there are 64 million empty homes in China's Ghost Cities. And believe it or not, as many as 28 more have been planned across the country.

♖

NOW I ADMIT, from the outside looking in, what's going on in China seems like the biggest real estate bubble in history. But just like in all the events of the modern Great Game, the real story is actually something *much* different.

In this case, it overlooks the greatest urbanization story the world has ever seen. In 2011, the urban share of the Chinese population passed 50% for the first time, reaching 51.3%. That compares to 1980 when 20% of the population lived in cities.

But this trend toward urbanization has a long way to run. According to OECD projections, China's urban population is set to expand by more than 300 million by 2030. That's almost equal to the entire population of the U.S. With 15–20 million people migrating to cities each year, China simply cannot afford to sit back and wait. Given the scale of the movement, it won't be long before China needs each and every one of these Ghost Cities.

In fact, this is all part of China's bigger strategy as it modernizes its economy.

A McKinsey study estimates that by 2025, China will have more than 220 cities with populations in excess of one million, versus 125 in 2010, and that 23 mega-cities will have a population of at least five million.

So essentially, the Chinese are thinking three moves ahead on the chessboard.

You aren't looking at a real estate bubble, because, put simply . . .

China isn't building for *today*; China is building for *tomorrow.*

These Ghost Cities represent just one phase of an incredible plan China has put into motion, which will become evident to all Americans in the years to come.

China isn't just building Ghost Cities. China is building an Empire.

Now, if you're in the empire-building business, and China most definitely is, you need to create strategic alliances—to solidify your key place on the chessboard of the Great Game.

And that's exactly what China's been doing to perfection. And it's crystal clear what these alliances are allowing them to secure: access to resources and the infrastructure that supports it all.

This fact is never more apparent than in the energy markets, where "The Dragon" remains unquenchable.

After all, China is no different than any other nation in the world when it comes to energy. It requires massive amounts of power to keep it all going. Without it, its "economic miracle" would wither on the vine.

Simply put, China needs energy in the same way that its babies need rice. As the Chinese economy grows, power consumption must grow right along with it.

And unlike the U.S., where energy usage peaked in the last bubble, China's per capita energy usage still has a ton of room to grow. That's because by comparison, the average Chinese consumer burns five times less energy annually than the average American does, leaving nothing but upside as the Chinese workforce consistently consumes more.

Today, China is the world's number one energy consumer, surpassing the U.S. in 2009, according to the Paris-based International Energy Agency.

It's a pattern that will continue, even if their economy begins to "slow."

Keep in mind that 5% annual growth for them would be considered a downturn. Meanwhile, the U.S. economy will likely remain stuck in the ditch for some time, growing by just over 3%.

And ever since China became an energy importer in 1993, it has adopted a "go out" strategy to secure energy assets abroad.

That's why China's investment in Africa has increased 30-fold since 2005. So where have they focused all of that money?

Well, those Ghost Cities they were building inside their own country? They've begun constructing them in Angola, too.

Outside of Angola's capitol, Luanda, is the Ghost City Nova Cidade de Kilamba. It's built across 12,355 acres and currently has 750, eight-story apartment buildings, a dozen schools, 100 retail stores, and is built to house 500,000 people.

But like all the others, Nova Cidade de Kilamba is empty. It's a $3.5 billion Angolan Ghost City, paid for by the Chinese. And there are several others just like it being built as well.

So why would China be willing to foot these bills? It's simple: Angola is China's largest oil supplier in Africa. By building these Ghost Cities for Angola, China is making a strategic ally in this country, while securing their energy future.

It's the same story in Nigeria. Only, China isn't building a "Ghost City" there. Instead they're building an airport financed with a 2% interest rate and a 22-year repayment period.

When describing this sweetheart deal, Nigeria's Aviation Minister Stella Oduah said *"it's almost free money."*

Of course, that "free money" came with two important catches:

1. **Nigeria is boosting their oil supplies to China from 20,000 barrels a day to 200,000.**
2. **They've agreed to dump an enormous portion of the US dollars in their reserves and convert them into a large stake in yuan.**

But the Chinese Government isn't stopping in Africa. The China Development Bank (CDB) and Export-Import Bank of China are lending billions of yuan to some of the world's riskiest regimes at interest rates several percentage points below the cheapest commercial loans available at home.

Recenty in Latin America, China's then-President Xi Jinping pledged to lend US$3 billion to 10 Caribbean countries, CDB offered a US$900 million loan to build a refinery in Costa Rica, and Mexican oil company Petroleos Mexicanos received a US$1 billion line of credit from China Eximbank.

And while the U.S. fought a prolonged war in Iraq, China secured a deal to develop the Rumalia oil field which is responsible for a third of Iraq's total oil output. China National Petroleum Corporation (CNPC) is now one of the largest foreign companies, in terms of production, operating in Iraq.

And they did it without putting a single troop in harm's way.

You name them . . . Brazil, Turkey, the United Arab Emirates, even our allies in U.K. and Japan—China has formed similar strategic alliances with each of these nations as well.

Perhaps most shocking, is what China is doing right here in North America. In fact, since 2009, almost half of the capital Chinese oil companies have spent on overseas mergers and acquisitions has been used to purchase assets in North America.

In the United States alone, Chinese oil companies have invested more than $8 billion since 2010.

Yet, it's the moves in its own backyard that are perhaps the most significant. Enabled in part by the Shanghai Cooperation Organization (SCO), China is building a maze of overland pipelines, roads, and railways in a modern version of the old "Silk Road."

China's ultimate goal is to become better connected to its Middle Eastern oil suppliers overland through Mackinder's Central Asian "Heartland." Given the U.S naval presence in the area, Beijing has become increasingly hesitant to rely on its maritime routes, making pipelines a better option.

Established in 2001, the SCO consists of China, Russia, Kazakhstan, Kyrgyzstan, Tajikistan, and Uzbekistan, along with four other observer states, Iran, Pakistan, India, and Mongolia. Over the years, China has used this organization to create better economic integration with its Central Asian trading partners, projecting Chinese hegemony over Eurasia.

In particular, China is working to create dependency in Central Asia using oil and gas deals along with various political and military agreements.

All of this, of course, takes not only resources, but cash—and China has more money than it knows what to do with. Along the way, they've become a formidable financial superpower.

In fact, China has more money in foreign reserves than Brazil, Russia, India, and South Africa combined.

According to the People's Bank of China (PBOC), China's foreign exchange reserves hit US$3.95 trillion at the end of March 2013. That's up US$509.7 billion from the end of 2012. As a net creditor the world, China also holds about $1.3 trillion worth of U.S. treasuries.

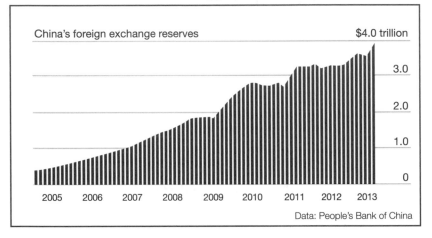

The World's Biggest Pile of Cash

It's the largest currency reserve stockpile that has ever been amassed. And keep in mind, China's foreign exchange reserves totaled around US$100 billion in 1996.

What's more, that's now, *after* an empty Paris and nearly 30 other Ghost Cities have been built.

And in addition to stockpiling massive exchange reserves, China has built up an enormous stake in physical gold as well, which as we'll learn later has massive implications for the U.S. dollar.

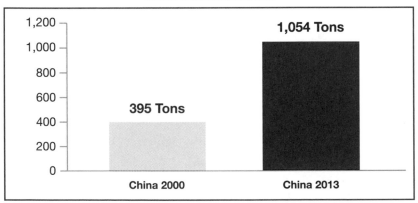

China's Gold Reserves

In 2000, their gold reserves sat at 395 tons. Today, that figure is 167% higher. China's central bank now has 1,054 tons of gold. And this will only speed up. That's because since 2009, China has acquired controlling stakes, or outright ownership, in no less than $2.1 billion worth of gold mines.

Thanks to aggressive moves in Indonesia, Canada, the U.K., and Australia, they're now the world's most dominant gold producer. And their largest gold miner has committed to spending at least $1.6 billion a year on international acquisitions moving forward.

So while the U.S. has been slowly experiencing the inevitable decline that comes from an empire that has overextended itself with too much debt, China is making one of the most unbelievable transformations in the history of the world.

It's like two ships passing in the night. The "Setting Sun Syndrome" that destroyed the British Empire at the turn of the previous century is weakening America's Empire now.

And, it's allowing China to establish a foothold as an unstoppable worldwide superpower.

That's given China the kind power it hasn't had in centuries. And it's not afraid to flex its muscles either—especially in its own back yard.

6

China Casts an Eye to the East

"THE MAN WHO REMOVES A MOUNTAIN BEGINS BY CARRYING AWAY SMALL STONES"

— CHINESE PROVERB

CHINA'S MASSIVE GROWTH story has caused it to make a pivot of its own. Beyond its moves in the Heartland, China is making a giant play in its Eastern "backyard."

In fact, if a global energy war explodes, smoldering tensions in the South China Sea would be the most likely catalyst.

Admittedly, China has built one of the world's largest economies by developing its own natural resources and partnering with other countries. But China's ambitions go well beyond sharing profits with other countries, or drilling, digging, pumping, and processing within its own borders.

In the Great Game, Beijing now believes one of its trump cards involves the islands and waters that are outside—in some cases well outside—of mainland China.

Its Southeast Asian neighbors disagree, especially in Japan, Taiwan, and the Philippines. For that matter, so does the U.S.

Add in simmering tensions and cultural slights that date back to pre-World War II, accusations of Nazi-like tactics, and billions in potential oil and gas riches, and it's no wonder that tensions in this area have reached a boiling point.

Territorial Disputes in the South China Sea

This map depicts disputed islands in the China Sea, as well as the conflicting territory claims.

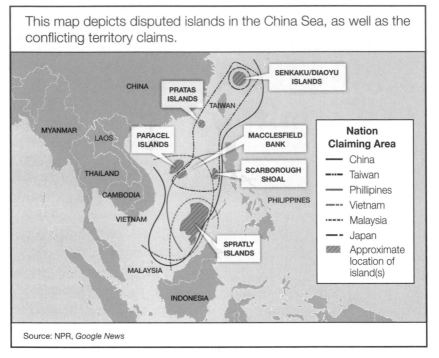

Source: NPR, *Google News*

While most Americans have little idea of the struggle that is taking place in these waters, the stakes couldn't possibly be higher.

The new "theater of war" is the South China Sea, which contains a series of disputed islands and potentially huge reserves of oil and natural gas. The latest activities there would make a great movie: military build-ups, back channel diplomacy, fiery speeches, saber-rattling, huge fortunes, empire building and globetrotting presidents and envoys.

But this isn't Hollywood. It's a dispute over who will prevail in Southeast Asia, and possibly the rest of the world.

Bounded by the South China Sea, in an area known as the "cow's tongue," here are the players—and their disputes.

There's the Scarborough Shoal, which is claimed by China, the Philippines, and Taiwan. There's also the Pratas Islands, claimed by China and Taiwan. The Paracel Islands are claimed by China, Taiwan, and Vietnam. The Macclesfield Bank is claimed by China, Taiwan, Vietnam, and the Philippines. And the Spratly Islands are claimed by China, Taiwan, Vietnam, Malaysia, the Philippines, and Brunei, a tiny sultanate.

This region is flush with energy resources, though estimates into how much oil and natural gas lies beneath the seafloor varies. The region is also critical to manufacturing and trading, with a significant portion of the world's products traveling through the region daily. There's also a rich fishing ground that employs thousands and feeds millions.

Obviously, China wants—and actually needs—those energy resources so it can continue along its torrid growth path. Beijing believes China's emergence as the dominant player in the region means it should have control over the islands, the seaways that surround them, and the rich resources they would bring . . . whether that control violates international and maritime law or not.

Beijing has rebuffed all attempts to have this morass of claims negotiated in a "multilateral" setting, such as group talks with the members of the Association of Southeast Asian Nations (ASEAN). Instead, it wants any negotiations to take place "bilaterally"—between it and one other nation at a time.

In Western terms, this would be a "divide and conquer" strategy, as China systematically overpowered its smaller, weaker neighbors one by one.

Meanwhile, the conflicts have intensified.

China has moved to effectively cordon off the horseshoe-shaped Scarborough lagoon, making it off-limits to fishermen from the Philippines, just 120 miles away. Yet in 1982, The Third United Nations Conference on the Law of the Sea defined a country's Exclusive Economic Zone (EEZ) as a band extending 200 miles from shore.

China also established a prefecture-level city called "Sansha" on Woody (Yongxing) Island, the largest in the Paracel and Spratly group, through which it will "administer" those islands, as well as the Macclesfield Bank.

Soon after, Beijing said it would install a military garrison on that island. Some observers said it was largely an administrative move—more symbolic than substantive—and dismissed any arguments to the contrary as "saber-rattling." Neighboring countries view the garrison as provocative.

China and its neighboring nations desperately want the energy resources beneath the South China Sea, and the dispute has caught the attention of global financial markets.

Long a critical world trade route and a strategically important region, the resources in the South China Sea are a strategic asset the booming region needs to sustain its growth.

The U.S. Energy Information Administration (EIA) projects total liquid fuels consumption in Asian countries outside the Organization for Economic Cooperation and Development (OECD) to rise by 2.6% a year, growing from approximately 20% of world consumption in 2008 to over 30% by 2035. Meanwhile, China has set an ambitious target of increasing the share of natural gas in its energy mix from 3% to 10% by 2020.

China's biggest offshore oil company, CNOOC Limited, estimates that the area could hold 17 billion tons of oil and 498 trillion cubic feet of natural gas. China's Ministry of Land and Resources says the area contains more than 40 billion tons of oil equivalent.

Most of that is believed to be in the form of natural gas. The EIA estimates the South China Sea contains approximately 11 billion barrels of oil and 190 trillion cubic feet of natural gas in proved and probable reserves.

According to the U.S. Geological Survey (USGS), the region's unexplored areas could contain an additional 5–22 billion barrels of oil and 70–290 trillion cubic feet of gas, though it's unclear how feasible it would be to extract them. Another Chinese estimate says 2,000 trillion cubic feet of natural gas lie under the South China Sea, which would be enough gas to meet the country's needs for centuries.

Like most offshore oil projects, the conditions in the South China Sea would make for difficult operations even without the territorial disputes.

Paradoxically, considering the region's conflicts, an expedition which is part of the 2013–2023 International Ocean Discovery Program (IODP) sent a team of scientists from 10 different countries to explore for oil and natural gas at a greater depth under the seafloor than ever before.

Proving that the quest for energy makes for strange bedfellows, scientists from China, Taiwan, and the U.S. were onboard the ship: 13 from mainland China, nine from the U.S., and one from Taiwan. The Chinese government paid 70% of the cost.

But to assume that a cooperative scientific expedition is a forerunner to government, trade, and energy exploration cooperation would be a mistake. If the group indeed finds oil deposits, the diplomatic stakes will be high for the countries vying for control of the South China Sea waterways and islands.

Adding to the uncertainty is that much of the known reserves lie under the shallow waters surrounding the disputed islands. This may make extraction easier, but it further complicates the territorial and ownership disputes.

Perhaps because of that, China has advanced into deep-water areas in the Pearl River Mouth and Qiongdongnan basins, areas which are farther from the many islands that dot the sea. Brunei, Malaysia, Indonesia, and Thailand have drilled in the region, and the Philippines and Vietnam have begun explorations.

Meanwhile, Singapore has established a major transit point and a refining center in the region. According to the *Oil & Gas Journal*, Singapore now has a crude refining capacity of 1.4 million barrels per day.

But this exploration has been hampered because many major international oil companies, who would be skilled partners in exploring for and extracting oil and gas, are avoiding involvement in the ongoing territorial disputes.

In fact, China has already successfully pressured companies like BP plc and Exxon Mobil Corp. to abandon their deals with neighboring Vietnam. Although some partnerships have been formed between companies and countries, several major energy firms have chosen to remain on the sidelines.

CNOOC itself caused a diplomatic row with Vietnam when it put up for auction nine oil and gas blocks that Vietnam claims are in its territory. These same blocks had already been auctioned by Vietnam to companies including ExxonMobil and Russia's Gazprom.

Meanwhile, the Filipino government has moved to have international authorities declare China's claims in the region "illegal and invalid."

Along the way, Chinese and Japanese fighter jets have had several dangerous engagements in the air over the disputed islands. And Vietnam has charged that a Chinese fishing boat slashed a seismic cable attached to an oil-and-gas exploration ship in the Gulf of Tonkin, claiming this was the latest deliberate attempt aimed at keeping the small nation from discovering new energy deposits.

As a result, Vietnam and India have stepped up naval patrols in the region, and the Philippines have announced plans to send more warships. For the first time, the Vietnamese publicly acclaimed the date a naval battle fought against China over disputed islands 40 years ago, shortly after the Chinese government announced new rules that required foreign fishing vessels to seek China's permission to operate in much of the South China Sea.

Taiwan called those same rules "state piracy."

In response, Vietnam has taken delivery of its first Russian-made Kilo class submarine, which is part of a substantial military upgrade by Hanoi. Malaysia has added two French-made Scorpene submarines, boosting its own maritime capabilities. For their part, Indonesia and Singapore are also expanding their fleets.

As part of this arms race, you can bet the growing wealth in Southeast Asia will give the countries involved even more resources to spend on ships, submarines, weapons, troops, and all the other components of armed conflict.

And, just to ratchet up the tension further, Philippine then-President Benigno Aquino compared China's expansion plans to those of Nazi Germany prior to World War II.

But infighting among the non-Chinese members of ASEAN has meant that attempts to present a united front opposing potential Chinese expansion have failed. With each apparently seeking the largest possible share of the oil and gas reserves beneath the surface of the South China Sea, there appears to be little interest in forming even an uneasy alliance with its neighbors.

♜

INTO THIS POWDER keg has stepped . . . the United States.

Toward the end of his first term, President Barack Obama announced that the U.S., which had long concentrated on diplomatic ties with European nations, was going to "pivot" towards Asia. U.S. diplomats and military envoys, followed by then-President Obama himself, made multiple trips to Asian countries, seeking to bolster relationships, trade agreements and other partnerships.

Some of those relationships are, of course, with China, which has become an increasingly important U.S. trading partner. Many U.S.

technology firms produce their products in huge factories in China, Malaysia, and other Asian countries.

Even still, the first tentative U.S. steps in the region involved sending 2,500 Marines to a base in northern Australia, which caught China's attention. Then, the U.S. began building closer ties by beginning the process of negotiating the Trans-Pacific Partnership (TPP), a free trade agreement that links a number of Asia-Pacific countries.

These smaller Asian countries recognize that the U.S. is the only country with enough muscle to stand up to China, which is why the Philippines allowed the U.S. to send military forces to the Naval Base in Subic Bay in Olongapo, Zambales, Philippines for the first time in almost 20 years.

The move is the first step of a newly signed 10-year agreement between the U.S. and the Philippines. The agreement, which marks a reversal for the Philippines, does not include new U.S. bases in the country, but will bring American ships and planes to the Philippines more frequently, and include more joint-training exercises. Although militant protesters see the U.S. as no better than China, Philippine officials appear to recognize the value of American military might in the region.

And it's not just about energy. More than half of the world's annual merchant fleet tonnage passes through the Straits of Malacca, Sunda, and Lombok, with much of it continuing on to the South China Sea. In fact, almost a third of global crude oil and over half of all global liquefied natural gas (LNG) passes through the South China Sea, making it one of the most important trade routes in the world.

So make no mistake—this situation can and will affect the United States.

First, if it succeeds in grabbing and holding the China Sea region and all its treasures, China will preclude any chance the U.S. might have had at accessing those resources had they been harvested by the Philippines, Japan, or even Vietnam, which seems glad to have the U.S. involved in this fracas right now.

Second, a China-controlled South China Sea could impact the navigation paths of both commercial shipping, and the U.S. Navy. That's no small item, especially since it could inhibit the U.S. Navy's ability to move freely in that region.

In the Great Game, the moves, countermoves, alliances, feints, and fake-outs in this area of the world are almost dizzying. Shifting alliances are almost a weekly occurrence, and new potential threats are as frequent as they are unpredictable.

That's why many international experts see this region as being one of the most likely to set off a future conflict in the world. Even so, it continues to be badly underestimated by the "experts" and the U.S. news media.

Unfortunately, that risk just keeps escalating.

But China's aggressive move to the East extends well beyond the South China Sea. China has players and pieces on almost every continent—even in our own backyard.

7

China's Claim to America's Backyard

"PERSISTENCE CAN GRIND AN IRON BEAM
DOWN TO A NEEDLE."
— CHINESE PROVERB

♜

FOR THE KNIGHTS Templar, a bloodthirsty, pseudo-religious drug cartel in western Mexico, drug trafficking is no longer its top source of income.

Instead, the cartel smuggles something else the world is much more desperate for. It's a scheme so large and bold, it's led to clashes with the Mexican Navy and a takeover of the port of Lázaro Cárdenas in the western state of Michoacan.

The material is iron ore. The desperate customer is China.

According to Mexican authorities, drug cartels began infiltrating the mining industry in 2010, with extortion, kidnapping, and piracy as their main weapons. They found a willing customer in the Chinese, who were (and are) desperate for the raw materials fueling their economic expansion.

The Chinese Foreign Ministry has refused to comment on whether it has any measures in place to ensure that the iron ore it receives from Mexico is legally obtained.

Throughout Mexico and the rest of Latin America, China has moved aggressively to expand its network of energy and natural resource suppliers, almost regardless of who those suppliers are—to the point that the Asian giant now owns the oil production of an OPEC member.

Once considered untouchable by non-U.S. interests, the former "backyard of the United States" is now increasingly coming under Chinese control, leaving environmental disasters, lawsuits, suspected corruption, shattered alliances, and double-crosses in its wake.

In the Great Game, Latin America now appears to be turning into a Chinese pawn.

In 2012, Chinese President Xi Jinping toured Latin America and the Caribbean. "The Latin America and Caribbean region is one of the most dynamic and promising regions in the world," he noted, while commenting that his goal was to deepen China's relations with the region.

Home to two members of OPEC (Ecuador and Venezuela), as well as 20% of the world's known underground oil reserves, Mexico and other Latin American countries have drawn the attention of every major oil company and player in the Great Game for the region's rich natural and energy resources. From Mexico in the north, to Argentina in the south, no one appears to have more influence than the Chinese.

Centuries ago, the invaders were from Spain, France, and other European nations, seeking territory and riches like gold. But this time, the invaders are from North America and Asia, as well as Europe. And they seek not gold, but black gold: The vast oil reserves that lie under North and South America, as well as natural gas, minerals, and other natural resources.

In Mexico, the authorities have welcomed the "invaders," though not the drug cartels, with open arms.

After operating as a monopoly for 76 years, Mexico is now set to dismantle all the barriers to foreign investment in its oil fields.

It started when the current President, Enrique Peña Nieto, was sworn into office on December 1, 2012. One of his major initiatives promised big reforms in PEMEX, the nationalized and state-run oil/gas producer, as well as the energy sector as a whole.

That required a revision of the national constitution and a slew of new laws. But in the end, these changes have been approved, at least in outline.

Now admittedly the "devil is in the details," but the potential upside for energy investors is significant.

These reforms will open the doors to outside companies and investments, provide the basis for joint ventures and other initiatives, and introduce the Mexican energy market to international services and support—all for the first time since the sector was nationalized on March 18, 1938.

Given that the country has substantial known reserves, there's already plenty of American interest. According to the latest U.S. Energy Information Administration (EIA) figures, Mexico is ranked sixth in shale gas and seventh in tight/shale oil in the world. Mexico has technically recoverable shale resources of 545 trillion cubic feet (cf) of natural gas and 13.1 billion barrels of crude oil and condensate.

Today, there are no fewer than five major basins to develop, and the most promising—the Burgos basin—is actually an extension of the highly productive Eagle Ford basin in South Texas, with well-defined geology and reserve estimates.

Further to the south and east, the shale geology of the onshore Gulf of Mexico basin becomes structurally more complex and the shale development potential is less certain. Nonetheless, the Sabinas basin has an estimated 124 trillion cf of risked, technically recoverable shale gas resources within the Eagle Ford and La Casita shales. The problem is the basin is faulted and folded, which means there are technical challenges in locating and extracting shale gas.

More favorable structures include the Tampico, Tuxpan, and Veracruz basins that stretch out in the east near the Gulf as you move further south in Mexico.

These basins are expected to add another 28 trillion cf and 6.8 billion barrels of risked, technically recoverable shale gas and shale oil potential from the same prolific source rocks that have provided Mexico's conventional onshore and offshore fields in this area for years. Still, there's been no serious exploratory drilling here.

The fact that there are already U.S. operating companies, field services, support, and expertise just north of the border has hardly gone unnoticed.

Another priority involves the major need for new investment and technology to reverse the declining production curve in Mexico's once dominant onshore and offshore oil fields.

PEMEX has made some progress in arresting what had been a precipitous collapse in production. But significant time and field pressure has already been lost. Reversing this trend—upon which the national economy is still dependent—requires money and equipment that is only available from the outside.

♜

IN ECUADOR, THE situation is just the opposite. Only one major player has received an invitation to "play" in the country's oil fields: China.

China, in essence, bought its way in.

The Pacifico Project, known locally as the Refineria, is a $13 billion, 300,000 barrel per day complex slated to begin operations in 2017.

The Pacifico Project will be built by Chinese Sinopec—Sinopec Shanghai Petrochemicals—while processing about 16% of its capacity in heavy oil from Venezuela. It's also being primarily funded by Beijing and will have the China National Petroleum Corp. (CNPC) as a partner.

This move into Ecuador and other South American venues mirrors similar moves in other parts of the world and is driven by Chinese finance.

With this deal, China now controls Ecuadorian crude oil production.

Put another way, Beijing can now dictate where the oil exports are going from a member of OPEC. To be sure, Ecuador is the smallest producer in the cartel, about 500,000 barrels a day.

Even so, the symbolism is dramatic.

This was accomplished because of the continuing financial difficulties faced by President Rafael Correa's administration. The nation defaulted on $510 million of foreign bonds in 2008, terming the debt "immoral" and "illegitimate." Investors lost everything, and international lenders became leery of ever lending the country money again. That allowed China to move in, offering funds at relatively high interest rates with Ecuador having few genuine alternative sources.

The collateral for the loans was Ecuador's oil industry.

Beijing has loaned billions to the government budget, the national oil company PetroEcuador, bankrolled the primary hydroelectric power project in the country, and is now about to finance one of the largest refineries in South America. Ecuador pays back these loans from the proceeds of its oil exports.

And the Chinese are rather creative in how that works out.

Only a relatively small amount of the country's oil exports actually go directly to China. In fact, PetroEcuador still depends on selling most of its oil closer to home to U.S. and other North American companies, either receiving the shipments or having control over the contracts.

Nonetheless, anecdotal evidence, shipping manifests, and intelligence from sector sources point toward a Chinese control of up to 90% of the oil leaving Ecuador.

This is hardly the first time China has used loans to gain leverage over South American oil.

Chinese state banks have loaned more than $10 billion to Brazil and over $40 billion to Venezuela. Hydrocarbons are the essential collateral in each case.

Two Chinese State-owned oil giants, China National Offshore Oil Corp and China National Petroleum Corp, are part of a consortium (including Royal Dutch Shell, France's Total SA and Brazil's state oil company Petrobras) that were awarded a 35-year production sharing contract to develop Libra, a deep-water oilfield off the Rio coast estimated to hold up to 12 billion barrels of oil.

These parallel similar steps by the Chinese elsewhere—at least $13 billion to Angola, upwards of $20 billion in Sudan, and a whopping $55 billion in Russia.

Add to this the acquisitions in the region, such as the recent purchase of Petrobas' assets in Peru and a cross-border pipeline project, and China's goal to develop an integrated presence in South America is rapidly reaching fruition.

Yet to accomplish this Chinese companies need larger positions as operators upstream. China's Sinopec Shanghai Petrochemical Co., Ltd. is already doing so in Ecuador, despite its primary experience being in refining.

The Ecuadorian government plans to develop the Ishpingo, Tambococha, and Tiputini (ITT) oil block, pitting the state against environmentalists, indigenous populations, and a wide swath of the scientific community.

This block is inside the Yasuni National Park, a UNESCO global biosphere area, the nation's largest nature reserve, and the home of two indigenous tribes wanting nothing to do with the outside world. Unfortunately, those tribes are "sitting" on some of the region's largest oil reserves.

The government has responded by closing the offices of a highly visible environmental group, claiming they have been fomenting violence. Meanwhile, the prospect of some 900 million barrels of crude continues to generate considerable interest.

Chinese companies are now positioning themselves to take a major chunk, despite the fact the project is "officially" being run by Petroamazonas, a unit of state oil company Petroecuador, and not the government itself. On the other hand, any approach will need to be very carefully orchestrated, given the environmental fallout from another matter about to come back into the news.

The more than two decade-old legal fight between Chevron and the Ecuadorian government over massive pollution in the rain forest region of Oriente is heating up again. It was one of the most horrendous ecological disasters I've ever seen.

Initially, the development upstream there was by Texaco (later absorbed by Chevron), with claims being waged between the American company and Petroecuador over who was really responsible for cleanup.

In its wake, a Chevron countersuit filed in a New York federal court came down against Ecuador. The liability here is now approaching $10 billion with a major judgment against the company already handed down in Ecuador.

The ITT development is now bringing back the same ecological concerns and adding fuel to an already tense situation. Foreign companies, certainly the Chinese, are going to need to walk a tightrope.

In the past, Correa has successfully championed environmental attacks against Western interests as a political tool, using them to condemn Chevron while pairing with the Chinese.

But his strong support for the ITT project may come back to dent his political image.

♖

THIS IS QUICKLY escalating into a major test of how sophisticated the Chinese have become in the geopolitics of oil.

Further south in Argentina, the Great Game centers around a different source of oil—shale.

There, several basin structures have all the earmarks of becoming huge producers. In this case, the government has nationalized the primary designated producer by controlling 51% of the shares in YPF S.A.

China has declared shale gas development as a top priority, and has been identifying the first locations for drilling, with some significant and ongoing help from the Unconventional Gas Technical Engagement Program (UGTEP), a U.S. Department of State program first called the Global Shale Gas Initiative.

In what's already being viewed as the most significant Western Hemisphere shale agreement outside North America, Chevron announced it has entered into a $1.24 billion project to produce both shale gas and tight oil with YPF.

The target is a basin called Vaca Muerta (literally "Dead Cow"), believed to hold as much as 23 billion barrels of oil equivalent.

The Vaca Muerta Shale: Argentina's Mother Load

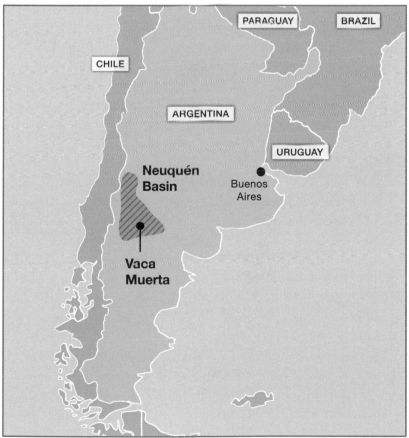

First stage development of the 50-50 joint venture will involve 100 wells providing 50,000 barrels of oil and 3 million cubic meters (106 million cubic feet) of gas in daily production by 2017. The second stage anticipates 1,500 wells. Overall investment commitments could reach more than $15 billion before 2020.

But before that happens, the project faces significant legal hurdles.

That's because the state nationalization of YPF came at the expense of the company's former owner—Spanish major Repsol S.A.

After Repsol sued, Buenos Aires agreed to pay the company $5 billion for the seizure.

So far, Chevron has indicated they will move forward with the project. For its part, YPF is bringing in some other deep projects to fund development at Vaca Muerta—Dow Chemical and Bridas. The latter just happens to be a venture of local investors and China National Offshore Oil Corporation If this seems like a tangled web of shifting alliances, it is. And the stakes are high.

Venezuela alone has the world's third largest proven oil reserves . . .

And that's not even including the over 500 billion barrels of "heavy" crude that's estimated to be in the vast, mostly offshore Orinoco Belt.

They're also ranked 7th in the world in proven natural gas reserves.

Brazil is home to the 15th largest conventional crude oil reserves in the world.

In just their ultra-deep-water "pre-salt" fields alone, there are over 100 billion barrels—enough to service 14 years' worth of U.S. consumption.

And production from these fields is expected to more than triple by 2020.

Ecuador, a leading source of crude oil for America's west coast, is ranked 19th in proven oil reserves. Yet their oil infrastructure is developed enough to make them South America's fifth-biggest oil producer.

And they've almost doubled their domestic natural gas production in just the last year.

Argentina is 30th in the world rankings of proven oil reserves and 33rd in conventional natural gas. Yet they've just been upgraded to 2nd in the world in "estimated recoverable" shale gas reserves.

And recent estimates put their unconventional oil supplies at over 600 billion barrels.

There are also significant petro-resources, both conventional and unconventional, in Bolivia, Colombia, Chile, and Peru, while in Chile several Chinese companies, including Jia He Wei Ye, Golden Resource, Sky Solar, and the National Development Bank of China are investing in mining and solar power projects.

Chile, in fact, was the first Latin American country to sign a free trade agreement with Beijing.

In Colombia, China Petroleum and Chemical Corporation (Sinopec) partnered with the Indian Company ONGC to buy 50% of the Omimex de Colombia in 2006.

One obstruction has been an issue that isn't seen in the U.S.: kidnappings.

Revolutionary Armed Forces of Colombia—People's Army (or in Spanish: Fuerzas Armadas Revolucionarias de Colombia, also known as FARC) guerrillas have kidnapped Chinese oil workers, with intervention by the Colombian Army necessary to rescue them.

Besides kidnappings, union violence, roadblocks, and pipeline disruptions are not unusual.

Undaunted, ExxonMobil Exploration Co. Ltd is exploring for unconventional oil and gas in Colombia's Middle Magdalena basin. The supermajor will spend up to $45 million to test the Cretaceous La Luna formation.

Although staking a claim to the oil and gas reserves is a major strategic move in Latin America, it isn't the only game.

Transporting that energy is just as important as pumping it out of the ground.

Brazil, for example, is reaching out to its neighbors—and extending significant capital to forge new cross-country transportation routes for oil and gas to the ultra-lucrative Asian markets.

Another development is a new transcontinental pipeline project, which will be the largest in the world.

This will span the whole of South America, from top to bottom.

It's called the Gasoducto del Sur, also known as the Venezuela-Argentina Gas Line.

And it's slated to track through 5,000 miles of South American wilderness, from Venezuela to the southern tip of Argentina.

Significant funding will come, not from the U.S. or China, but from Russia, and the pipeline is completely blueprinted.

Russia, in fact, is looking to strengthen its influence in the region. Russian President Vladimir Putin has announced plans to set up military bases throughout South America, as well as increase arm sales there.

Published reports say Putin is looking to establish military bases in Cuba, Nicaragua, Peru, and Venezuela, including a major anti-narcotics training center in Nicaragua. The Russians have also discussed trade agreements with Costa Rica, Haiti, and Chile, and had talks with Brazil.

Despite that, the U.S. is still the biggest foreign investor in Latin America, with $41.5 billion in 2012.

In contrast, China's foreign investment overall hit a new high of $87.8 billion in 2012, according to a United Nations Economic Commission for Latin America and the Caribbean (ECLAC) study. Latin America accounted for 13% of that—about $11.4 billion in 2012, a significant increase from the $120 million of 2004. All told, between 2005 and 2013, China invested $102.2 billion in the region, according to Boston University.

Nowhere is the Great Game more complicated than in Latin America, where the promise of energy and natural resource riches have brought governments, energy companies, terrorists, and criminal organizations together in ways that would be unthinkable in much of the rest of the world.

Throughout the region, multiple projects, alliances and conflicts have the potential to be global game changers and affect nations and energy policies around the globe.

In the Americas, as in other continents, the power of each major player grows and shrinks with each new alliance, agreement, or double-cross resulting in a shifting of power.

Nowhere is that more obvious than in Eastern Europe and Asia, where the Russian bear has set its sights on world energy dominance.

8

The Russian Gambit

"RUSSIA IS A RIDDLE WRAPPED IN A MYSTERY INSIDE AN ENIGMA"

— WINSTON CHURCHILL

THE GREAT GEOPOLITICAL battle between nations for power and resources in the 21st century has many influential players. China is a heavyweight player in Eurasia, but it's far from the only one.

Despite having to take a back seat over the last 20 years, the Russian bear still has plenty of bite.

And just like in the 20th century, Russia's goal in the Great Game is to reestablish its dominance and boost its status over the course of the next century.

You may not know this, but I spent part of my career in Russia. I know the nation's history well. I know its strength and I know its weakness.

But back when I began my career, it was the dominant part of a sprawling Soviet Union.

Now, just two decades later, 15 independent countries stand in its place. And while Russia still casts a long shadow over Eastern Europe, it's hardly the bourgeoning empire it was in the 20th century.

But reality is a cruel master in the Great Game, especially when your moves are limited.

However, one thing is for certain, that won't stop Russia from trying to reassert itself as a big game player. It will aim to rise again as a major force in the global economy.

And central to Russia's Great Game strategy is a clever use of strengths known as "Pipeline Politics."

By using its vast natural resources and the pipelines that transport them as weapons, Russia is changing its attention from Western foes to Eastern allies, in a move that promises to rearrange the board.

And it all starts with one man: Vladimir Putin.

In this case, Putin represents the ultimate survivor mindset that's central to success in the Great Game. He's a fighter, and he'll do whatever it takes to keep his influence not only over Russia, but the world as well.

Putin will partner with a nation one day, and leave them high and dry the next. He will say one thing, and go in the opposite direction.

And that alone—forced anticipation of his unpredictability—is the type of power that the major players in the new Great Game have to account for in an interconnected global economy.

Since the collapse of the Soviet Union, Russia has struggled to build a diverse and robust economy.

Yet, the nation is still overly reliant on energy resource production to pay the bills, with 50% of its annual government revenues derived from oil and gas. This lack of diversification has stunted its long-term growth potential and contributed to ongoing stagflation.

In the big picture, the nation's inability (and unwillingness) to diversify its economy only hurts its economic might. It has also created a massive oligarchy of politically connected (and corrupt) business leaders (particularly in the energy industry) who rely on Putin's permission, influence, and grip on power.

But energy politics is all that Russia knows. As the Great Game unfolds, Russia must play its greatest card—using oil and gas to influence global politics and trade.

For two decades, Russia tried to shift to greater democratization, transparency, free markets, and cooperation with the West. And while the nation enjoyed some modest success, it wasn't entirely *Russian*.

But the last ten years have seen Putin turn away from cooperation, shifting toward political gamesmanship. Recent problems in Ukraine reflect the zero-sum Cold War mentality and the Pipeline Politics that are emerging in Putin's power dynamic.

Of course, at the time of the takeover of the Crimea region, President Barack Obama announced that the world is not a "cold-war chessboard in which we're in competition with Russia."

But what the President doesn't understand, is not everyone has given up on the Cold War. In Putin's mind, cooperation in geopolitics is, in fact, a zero-sum game that pits his nation against the West.

In fact, Putin's sentiment for the former Soviet Union was on display in 2005 when he said that its collapse "was the greatest geopolitical catastrophe of the century."

Said Putin back then, "First and foremost it is worth acknowledging that the demise of the Soviet Union was the greatest geopolitical catastrophe of the century. As for the Russian people, it became a genuine tragedy. Tens of millions of our fellow citizens and countrymen found themselves beyond the fringes of Russian territory."

As a result, his actions appear to be designed to return Russia to its golden years, and part of that involves defiance of the West.

For instance, since returning to power, Putin has downright refused to engage in aiding the West in talks with Iran over its nuclear ambitions. He has refused to allow a missile-defense shield in Eastern Europe, taking such suggestions of the project as a direct shot at Russia's government. What's more, with its vast energy supplies, Putin has even threatened to turn the lights off in Europe in order to assert his power position in the game.

This last action is a prime principle example of how Putin's Pipeline Politics work.

In April 2014, Putin threatened to stop gas flows to the energy-starved continent over a $2.2 billion energy debt from Ukraine. Some saw this as punishment for Ukraine's defiance and Europe's active recruitment to pull the Eastern nation into the European Union.

But for all the political theater, Putin's posturing hasn't helped Russia's economy, which is currently in a quagmire.

The decision to enter Ukraine is defined by Putin's manic desire to reestablish key portions of the Russian empire, all while moving his pieces on the global chessboard.

Sure, there were short-term consequences.

Russia's invasion of the Crimea region of Ukraine set off a geopolitical firestorm that led to problems for the Russian emerging market—a notable member of the BRIC countries (Brazil, India, and China comprise the rest). Russia's stock market tanked, thanks in part to swift outflows of capital and growing concerns about the impact of sanctions on some of its most notable businessmen and allies of Putin.

But despite these economic after-effects, Putin's Crimean "invasion" was remarkably popular among the Russian population.

This decision to invade the Crimea region reestablished nationalistic pride and, in the minds of the population, "saved" pro-Russian residents in the historic region that was once part of the Empire.

Crimea, which was heavily pro-Russia before the invasion, provides a strategic economic and military importance to Putin's vision. The Crimea region sits on the vital Black Sea, which hosts both Russia's Eastern Naval base and provides a direct trade route into the Mediterranean Sea.

The Crimea crisis also sets the table for Putin to make his next move. That move could be expansion into other parts of Ukraine, annexation of historic portions of Estonia, Finland, or Moldova.

But the aftermath of Putin's decision to enter Ukraine promises to have a profound impact on the nation's future, since it basically sets up a game of chicken with the West.

As it turns out, Russia's greatest strength in the Great Game could become one of its greatest weaknesses. The changing economic dynamics of the nation's most important sector, the energy market, could now threaten to undermine Putin's advance.

Oil and gas remain the basis for Russia's economic power and influence. But if Russia were one side of a chessboard, oil and gas would be the Rooks of the nation's power; the foundation, the stone walls of the nation's geopolitics.

But the game that was once central to its economic power has evolved, forcing Putin's hand at a time when global tensions are on the rise. Despite the Soviet downfall and lack of economic diversity, Russia has maintained leverage by becoming the largest non-OPEC producer of *conventional* oil.

The country's oil companies are able to exploit OPEC supply quotas to improve export pricing and undercut OPEC members in certain global regions to help Russian companies improve their market reach.

But that long-time leverage is now in jeopardy.

And it should be no surprise to find that it's the U.S. that has undermined Russia's energy dominance and created a new wrinkle in the 21st Century's Great Game.

Once again, it pits the U.S. directly against Russia.

The rise of unconventional energy resources like shale oil has turned the U.S. into an energy powerhouse. North American energy production now comprises 10% of global volume these days.

The U.S. is now on track to become the world's largest supplier, and it's a possible near-term reality.

Of course, Russia has campaigned against global expansion of unconventional sources. It has tossed out typical noise and misinformation to stop the American rise in oil and gas production.

Russia has even claimed that shale production is a "flash in the pan," an unsustainable venture.

But nations looking to break away from Russian dependence, especially across Europe, are considering the production of oil and gas from shale resources, or importing from shale-producing nations or producers of liquefied natural gas (LNG) like the U.S.

Thanks to the emergence of shale gas and LNG, Russia is no longer the only energy game in Europe.

And with Putin pushing hard on Ukraine, the EU is beginning to turn away from Russia. Countries like Germany have begun to push toward greater energy independence. The rest of Europe will follow.

The combination of imported LNG, rising local shale production, and renewable energy projects will make life difficult for Russia's energy giants Gazprom and Rosneft.

Meanwhile, these factors will hinder the Kremlin's geopolitical mobility back home due to its reliance on export revenues to fund the government.

♜

SO HOW DOES Russia respond? By using a two-tier strategy.

Since Putin returned to power in 2004, he has used the nation's vast energy resources as a strategic influence on Eastern Europe.

Of course, Russia is not the only country playing pipeline politics.

South American energy producer Venezuela has used its energy resources to reward new allies who defy the West. Meanwhile, China uses energy negotiations as a potential entry point for additional commodity agreements.

But nobody plays this aspect of the Great Game like Vladimir Putin.

For two decades, Russia's influence in Europe has been dominated by its supplies of oil and gas to Western nations. The company provided 24% of all energy consumed by the European Union's 28 nations in 2012.

Putin's Pipeline Politics

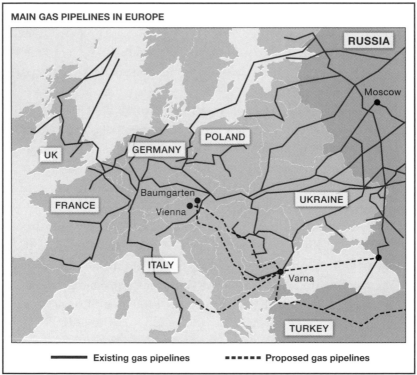

Four nations—Lithuania, Estonia, Finland, and Latvia—rely on Russia for 100% of their natural gas imports. Bulgaria, Slovakia, Hungary, Slovenia, and Austria all received more than 50% of their natural gas needs from the Eastern nation in 2012.

And Europe's most robust economy, Germany, imported 37% of its natural gas from Russia that same year.

Needless to say, Russia's influence on the region is dynamic, given that so many nations rely on them just to keep the lights on.

Everybody here remembers all too vividly the last Russian-Ukrainian spat. Back in January 2009, during one of the continent's coldest snaps in recent history, a disagreement broke out between Gazprom and the Ukrainian national gas company Naftogaz Ukrainy.

That resulted in a complete halt of the Russian gas pass-through across Ukraine, and some very cold folks further west. Now these concerns are surfacing again.

It's the equivalence of energy blackmail, with Putin using his pipelines that connect Russia to Europe like puppet strings to influence his Western neighbors.

But the events in Ukraine go beyond the symbolic. If Putin's not able to control Ukraine, Russia will lose its direct access to the West.

Though the energy revolution and greater independence is the goal of Europe, there's a short-term game to be played in the next few years as Russia and Europe decide who will blink first.

Russia will hope the unconventional oil revolution in Europe won't happen as fast as it did in in the U.S., while Western nations will push hard and fast, attempting to cut Putin's power out from underneath him.

In the near-term, though, Europe still needs Russia to pump fuel into the continent

♖

BUT PUTIN MIGHT think otherwise. Russia has now begun to turn its attention to new markets and new customers, possibly leaving Europe to suffer in the near-term, and hopefully for Putin, come crawling back to him for their much needed energy.

The good news for Russia is Asian nations desperately need energy sources to continue their absurd growth rates of the last two decades.

But Putin isn't just going to sell to Asia because he needs customers. With Russia, there's always an ulterior motive.

Putin and Russia will attempt to use pipeline development into Asia as a means of influencing the largest importer of oil in the world: China.

By diverting his resources to other nations like China, Japan, India, and the rest of the Far East, Putin is establishing new allies, heightening new tensions between the Old West and the New East.

But the truth is, the Russian-Ukrainian crisis is simply providing a central position for American energy trade moving forward. That trade will result in greater reliance by both continents on the U.S. as an energy-balancing factor. It will also result in better, more predictable pricing in Asia, and act as a counterweight to the increasing Russian exports via pipelines into the region.

That's hardly what the Kremlin had in mind when the situation in Crimea and Eastern Ukraine unraveled.

For Asia, a crisis elsewhere in the world is now providing an opportunity for better energy availability at home. But the new market will be driven by Russian gas coming by pipeline and U.S. LNG ferried in by tanker.

And that may just transport this new version of the Cold War to a whole different part of the world.

But "Pipeline Politics" aren't just about the actual flow of oil and gas to Asia. They also incorporate other elements of global trade.

Russia's second strategy in the Great Game is to target the West, and possibly weaken the leverage of the European Union and the U.S.

As we'll explore in the next chapter, Russia threatens the stability of the Western economy and the global currency used in energy trading.

Russia is cooperating with nations like Iran, Venezuela, China, and India to take down the petrodollar. For Putin, this move comes easily.

He has already labeled the U.S. influence on the global trade of oil a "parasite." So, Putin may consider attempting to hoard gold and establish trade of its oil to nations like India, China, and other nations feeling ignored by the U.S.-influenced International Monetary Fund in exchange for gold.

By applying pressure to the status of the petrodollar, Putin could have the ultimate trump card.

In fact, in May 2014, Putin visited China to establish trade ties with the world's largest economy. The nations have agreed on principle to trade oil and gas in a currency that is not the U.S. dollar.

And for good reason. Putin recognizes that China is now the world's largest importer of oil, and the largest trading nation. By aiding China in establishing its own currency into the global oil markets or facilitating a gold-backed oil system, Putin's answer to growing U.S. dominance in the oil markets could strike a significant blow to Western interests.

Undermining the petrodollar would be the equivalency of an economic nuclear strike on the Western economy, which has relied on dollar-based energy trading since 1973.

Would Putin go that far, or is he simply posturing? His unpredictability makes that question hard to answer.

In the meantime, you can expect Russia to stick to what's working. And one thing is certain: Putin's Pipeline Politics are popular at home.

Despite leading a nation on the brink of recession, foreign policy triumphs rally domestic support for Putin's initiatives. So long as Putin can humiliate the nation's age-old enemies in the West, the short-term ramifications of economic stagnation is tolerated by a nationalistic following.

After the Crimea takeover, his approval ratings jumped from their all-time low of 61% to nearly 70%.

It seems like Putin can increase that number by playing hard and fast in the Great Game.

9

The War on the U.S. Dollar

"I AM SADDENED THAT IT IS POLITICALLY
INCONVENIENT TO ACKNOWLEDGE
WHAT EVERYONE KNOWS: THE IRAQ WAR
IS LARGELY ABOUT OIL ."
— ALAN GREENSPAN

FOR OVER 43 YEARS, the United States has owned the most powerful piece on the Great Game board.

It's the luxury of owning the international economy's reserve currency, requiring buyers and sellers of crude oil to trade petroleum in American dollars and American dollars only.

This long standing arrangement has created a global currency known as the *petrodollar.*

It requires the international community to use American dollars, even at the expense of their own geopolitical self-interest in global trade.

By requiring the use of dollars, this system has created an insatiable demand for American greenbacks and, more importantly, U.S. debt around the globe.

For instance, Saudi Arabia, the world's biggest oil exporter, ploughs much of its earnings back into U.S. assets. Most of the Saudi central bank's net foreign assets of $690 billion are thought to be denominated in dollars, much of them in U.S. Treasury bonds.

This is what has allowed the U.S. to run up trillions of dollars of debt. The rest of the world uses their surplus of dollars to buy up debt in the form of U.S. interest-bearing securities.

As the world's only true superpower, this long-standing arrangement certainly has had its advantages.

Since 1971, the petrodollar has established U.S. economic, military, and political dominance.

But what happens when the rest of the world realizes that the U.S. is no longer at the top of the heap and decides to abandon the dollar in favor of gold or other currencies to boost their own fortunes?

In other words, what will happen when the rest of the world figures out they already have the biggest trump card of them all?

Well, you don't have to wonder any longer. Those days are already here.

In fact, there's a brewing war against the petrodollar right now. China, Russia, and a host of others have already come to the conclusion that "business-as-usual" is no longer their preferred method when it comes to conducting global oil transactions.

This could well be the most critical geopolitical issue that the U.S. faces over the next ten years, since a move away from the dollar threatens to unravel the nation's grip on its global economic power.

New developments mean the U.S. is now looking at the prospect of the end of the petrodollar's international standing. The implications of this move promise to be huge.

Of course, the reign of the petrodollar is rooted in the aftermath of World War II.

After the surrender of the Axis Powers in 1945, the U.S. was the only economic power standing that had the capacity to rebuild the world, particularly a war-torn Europe.

Near the end of the World War II, the 1944 Bretton Woods Conference established the U.S. dollar as the global reserve currency, enabling the U.S. to dethrone a debt-riddled and war-battered Great Britain as the world's economic super power.

The Bretton Woods Agreement created an international monetary system backed by the economic and political stability of gold, in addition to the global financial agency known as the International Monetary Fund.

For nearly two decades, this global system operated with the paper dollar tied to the underlying price of gold, since the international gold system forced global trading partners to use the greenback in all transactions of the metal as well.

But changing U.S. priorities of the 1960s eventually destabilized the dollar-to-gold system.

During the 1960s, the U.S. insisted on being a massive "Welfare State" that would distribute huge entitlements to its citizens. At the same time, the nation created a "Warfare State" that sent the U.S. into its long quagmire in Vietnam and established a global military presence around the world.

But eventually, the bill for Big Government expansion and the war machine of the 1960s came due.

The Bretton Woods system buckled under its own weight. In August 1971, President Richard Nixon ended the Bretton Woods Agreement that facilitated the dollar-to-gold agreement.

From that point forward, the U.S. dollar was no longer backed by gold. For the first time ever, the currency was allowed to float. In the aftermath, unhinging the greenback from gold led to a rapid devaluation of the dollar, along with higher than expected inflationary pressures.

Seeking to end the slide, the U.S. plotted a new way to maintain the stability of the dollar in international markets. Two years later, the U.S. found a new solution with the help of a Middle Eastern ally, even though the dollar had already lost some of its value.

In 1973, the U.S. asked Saudi Arabia to help it remain the global economic reserve currency by agreeing to only accept American dollars in exchange for Saudi Arabia's oil sales.

Now, if any nation wanted to purchase oil from Saudi Arabia, it first had to exchange its own currency for U.S. dollars in order to complete the transaction. This created an immediate global need for the greenback, and helped the U.S. drastically expand its debt capacity by ensuring that the world would always be flooded with dollars.

Just like that, the *petrodollar* was born. The greenback became America's number one export.

Sure enough, the U.S. was able to flex its geopolitical muscle, and, by 1975, all of OPEC agreed to accept only U.S. dollars in exchange for their oil.

But while the petrodollar flourished at first, the participants in this deal began to question the sanity of accepting a currency backed by *nothing* in exchange for their oil. For these reasons, OPEC needed something else to sweeten the deal.

They also sought military protection by the U.S. in addition to weapons and global intelligence against regional enemies. The U.S. agreed, fueling its global military expansion as the world's policeman.

A handful of nations, of course, have tried to move away from the dollar in their oil transactions over the years, including Venezuela, Syria, and Iran. Naturally, their geopolitical opposition to trading in any currency aside from the U.S. dollar has been met with reactions that range from harsh rhetoric and economic sanctions to long, drawn-out military actions.

One needs to look no further than military interventions over the last 15 years as evidence that the U.S. is willing to go to the ends of the earth to protect its financial interest.

♜

BUT THE WORST conflict could still be on the horizon.

Because when former Vice President Dick Cheney famously said, "The U.S. debt doesn't matter," he was only half-right.

It's not the debt that truly matters, but instead the currency upon which global powers base their trade upon. The soaring U.S. debt has grown under the assumption that the world would continue to rely on the petrodollar and use it in the vast portion of global trade.

In this case, it's not the debt that matters. It's the pulse of the *petrodollar.*

And although many Americans assume that the U.S. has gone to war or invaded other nations to help preserve freedom, expand democracy, or to eliminate despots, it has actually been focused on the preservation of the U.S. dollar as the world's reserve currency and basis of the global oil trade.

If you're unconvinced, simply look at the geopolitical actions of the U.S. over the last decade in two regional hotspots where crude oil is the core driver of those nations' economies: Iraq and Libya.

In 2001, Iraqi president (and dictator), Saddam Hussein, announced his intention to sell oil in a denomination other than the dollar. Instead, Hussein proposed a program to accept the Euro as a currency of preference in oil deals.

That Hussein had America at the top of his enemies list was not surprising. Neither was the reaction of the U.S. government. Swiftly, the heavy hand of U.S. military force entered Iraq, overthrew Hussein, and reestablished the dollar as the currency of choice.

The exact same pattern happened recently in Libya as well.

In 2010, then leader Muammar Gaddafi announced an oil-for-gold program (thus amassing billions in bullion wealth for the former dictator). Gaddafi quickly found himself the victim of a swift and brutal outcome. After his demise, Libya quickly reverted to its acceptance of the petrodollar.

Today only two key producing counties do not accept the dollar for oil. Syria pulled away from the petrodollar in 2006, while Iran moved away in 2008 creating its own International Oil Bourse (IOB). The IOB is an international exchange that allows international oil, gas, and petroleum products to be traded using a basket of currencies other than the U.S. dollar.

Since then, both nations have faced extensive economic sanctions, since the U.S. has never met an international force it could not overcome when it came to the preservation of the petrodollar.

That is until now.

Today, the U.S. dollar dominance could swiftly end as the Great Game unfolds.

It's very possible in the coming decades, years, or even months that Russia, China, India, Brazil, and other nations could turn away from the dollar and attempt to establish themselves as global economic powerhouses in the 21st century by eliminating the middle man.

In fact, they already believe they have the right—and more importantly, the reasons—to do so.

Since 2011, the BRIC nations have declared that Western dominance over the IMF exists to protect the West against the inevitable economic growth and expansion in the East. What's more these BRIC nations have issued multiple statements arguing that the IMF's continued commitment to only appointing Western leaders to run the agency undermines its legitimacy.

As a result, these nations are teaming up in the Great Game to position themselves against the West. They're even considering the creation of their own global economic agency to rival the power and might of the International Monetary Fund, a move that would rival

D-Day in terms of changing the balance of geopolitics. But this time, it would be the West that's attacked at dawn.

Nothing Lasts Forever . . . Not Even the U.S. Dollar

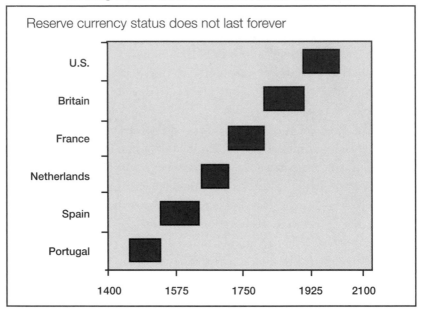

The question is, how far is the United States willing to go next in order to defend its dollar?

The truth is most Americans are largely unaware that Russia and China, two massive holders of U.S debt, have the potential to sink the U.S. financial system simply by refusing to use the petrodollar.

All either one of them has to do is commit to dealing in a currency or other means that isn't the dollar and never look back. And now it looks like they've set up a major petrodollar trigger over the next 18 months.

On March 2, 2014, a staggering announcement took place in Russia.

Andrei Kostin, the CEO of state-owned VTB bank, announced that Gazprom and Rosneft, the country's oil and gas giants, could begin trading fuels in the ruble in the very near future.

Meanwhile, Gazprom's CEO Alexander Dyukov all but confirmed a switch from the dollar, saying that 95% of his customers announced they were prepared to settle their energy debts in the euro.

But it gets even worse for the petrodollar.

In 2014, Rosneft signed a number of oil contracts with China and could also soon make such agreements with India. In these mega-contracts, no petrodollars would be exchanged. Instead, the nations would focus on establishing either gold as a primary trading instrument or a basket of regional currencies.

And the Great Game only promises to heat up from here. Russian President Vladimir Putin has said on multiple occasions that the U.S. has abused its economic superpower status due to the petrodollar's grip on global trade flows.

In 2011, Putin said that the U.S. was "like a parasite" in the global economy and claimed the petrodollar was a threat to the international financial system. Since then, Putin and Russia have begun to move against the U.S. dollar.

In recent years, Russia has more than doubled its gold reserves to more than 1,035 tons, comprising 8.3% of global reserves, according to IMF data. But it's not just Russia that's gobbling up the gold. China has dramatically increased its gold reserves in the last few years.

Though the nation has not reported its reserves since 2009, when gold reserves sat just above 1,000 metric tons, it's entirely possible that in just five short years, China has tripled its reserves. And a few estimates have even said that China could possibly have 7,000 tons, but they're simply underreporting their reserves.

All of this gold hoarding could very well be for one reason: To establish gold as a primary vehicle on which trade flows are built between emerging economies.

And the truth is, these nations have every reason to make the switch. In fact, there are real justifications to walk away from the petrodollar, a currency with nothing to back it except the value of the paper it's printed upon.

♖

TODAY, CHINA IS the world's second largest oil consumer, and the nation's thirst for energy is now so large that it actually imports more oil from Saudi Arabia than the U.S. does.

The reality is, it makes no logical sense that China is forced to collect U.S. dollars just so that it can purchase oil from its producers. The same thing goes for India, Indonesia, and a number of other oil-importing nations as well. It's simply inefficient to tie their trade to a currency with no security behind it.

Nor does it make any sense for immense oil producers like Brazil or Russia, the latter of which has already moved to sell its oil and gas in its own currency and gold in order to appease its customers.

Today, the Russian oil trade is more than $1 trillion annually. And if that market decided to abandon the U.S. dollar as its primary tool of trade, it would likely mark the end of the petrodollar.

Since the dollar would decline rapidly in that case, any nations with substantial holdings of U.S. dollars would be able to offset that decline by hedging with their massive gold reserves.

The West, however, would have to deal with the immediate aftermath.

The best-case scenario for the petrodollar's decline would be for the Federal Reserve to steadily re-peg the dollar to gold at an inflated price, and seamlessly transition the nation back to a gold-backed economy.

But that's not reality. The petrodollar's outright decline would be nasty.

For one, rampant inflation would be detrimental to exports, forcing the U.S. to engage in capital controls, as dramatic price increases would destabilize global commodity markets.

What's more, the U.S., which is sitting on $19 trillion in debt, would no longer be able to find willing customers for new debt without big increases in interest rates. Those same increases mean the U.S. economy would grind to a halt.

So while Americans and their government continue to think in the short-term world of the last 40 years, the other Great Game players are working to move the world in another direction.

Of course, how the war on the dollar plays out in the end remains to be seen. Empires never go down without a fight. Plus, you should never underestimate the power of the U.S.

As you'll see, the United States may be down, but it's far from being beaten.

10

Game-Changing Ingenuity

"THE PROBLEMS OF THE WORLD
CANNOT POSSIBLY BE SOLVED BY SKEPTICS
OR CYNICS WHOSE HORIZONS ARE
LIMITED BY THE OBVIOUS REALITIES.
WE NEED MEN WHO CAN DREAM OF THINGS
THAT NEVER WERE."
— JOHN F. KENNEDY

FEW WOULD LIKE to admit it, but the history of the modern Great Game is written largely in oil. From the Allied victory in World War II to the never-ending struggles in the Middle East, the quest for crude oil can be found at the center of it all.

You may not have read about it in your history textbooks, but oil has always played a major role, lurking as the story behind the story.

And if you read between the lines, you'll find oil everywhere you look. Dark and gooey, it's the single common thread that binds together the world as we know it.

But contrary to popular belief, the oil story didn't begin anywhere near a Texas oilman . . . The oil industry's roots are actually found in the Quaker State, otherwise known as Pennsylvania. It was there in 1859 that Edwin Drake first tried out his latest breakthrough, changing the world in the process.

His brainstorm? It was to drive a pipe down the well to keep the hole from caving in.

Seventy feet beneath the surface, in a place called Titusville, Colonel Drake hit pay dirt, making him the first person to ever successfully drill for oil. And with a single idea, the race for oil was born.

Soon after, speculators from all over the place began to gobble up land in the name of crude. One of them was a guy you might have heard of. His name was John D. Rockefeller, Sr.—the world's first billionaire.

Some 155 years later, a similar piece of American ingenuity is having that same exact effect, but now on a global scale.

It began with the inventiveness of another guy you've probably never heard of . . . His name is Richard L. Findley and without him, the Bakken Shale would be nothing but a big, dry hole.

At least that's what the majors such as Royal Dutch Shell, Gulf Oil, and Texaco Co. believed in the mid-90s when they packed up their gear and headed home.

But that didn't stop Findley from chasing a hunch. Undeterred, the geologist and "wildcatter" pressed on. And after scrutinizing years of old drilling records, it finally hit him—the big oil companies were simply drilling in the wrong direction.

According to Findley, instead of finding the oil-rich layers of the Bakken, they had mistakenly drilled right through them. In the process, they missed an underground river of high-quality crude.

"It was a light bulb kind of thought and I thought, 'My gosh, the oil is in the middle member,'" Findley said. "When I saw that this was continuous for 50 miles, I called my partner and I said, 'I think you'd better sit down. I think we found a giant oil field.'"

It was true: The mother lode of oil that had yet to be pumped. There were literally billions of dollars still in the ground. The bigger question, though, was how to pump it all out.

After all, drilling in the Bakken formation wasn't going to be easy as poking a hole in ground and hitting a soft spot full of oil. The Bakken's oil is bound up in a rock layer that's wide but thin.

Findley's idea was to drill a well sideways—using a technique called "horizontal drilling." A horizontal well drills down to the oil and then fans out thousands of feet to the side, like the piping for an underground sprinkler.

But it would take a lot more than Findley's horizontal drilling to start this oil boom.

Working with Lyco Energy Corp. and the drilling expertise of Halliburton, Findley's group finally hit pay dirt in May 2000 using a combination of horizontal drilling techniques and hydraulic fracturing.

The rest, as they say, is history. The "fracking" boom was born—and with it, another great oil rush.

But don't think for a minute this process is easy. For instance, take a look at these pumping trucks.

These are just *some* of the special trucks needed for a frack job.

Make no mistake: A working horizontal well is a massive display of parts, machinery, and know-how. In this case, we're looking at a medium-sized well site in the Marcellus, just over the line in northern West Virginia, where I was evaluating the footprint of the drilling pad.

Here's how it works.

First, the formations are mapped. Using 3-D seismic technology, layers of gas and oil are located and defined, giving the drillers solid targets and fewer dry holes.

Once mapped, a formation is drilled vertically first and then horizontally *into* the target layers rather than *through* them. That gives the

The picture above shows just a portion of what the pumping footprint at a small frack operation looks like.

well access to thousands of feet of resource, rather than the hundreds of feet typically encountered in a vertical well.

The next step is the key because shale is a "tight rock," making it difficult to extract without some serious help. As a result, the rock itself needs to be fractured or cracked all along the well before the oil or natural gas can flow from it.

To accomplish that, a water-chemical-sand mix typically is injected into the well under very high pressure. This pressure eventually exceeds the strength of the rock and it shatters, sort of like a broken windshield. That not only releases the oil and gas, but gives it a path to the production well.

Once fractured, a "propping agent" such as sand or ceramic beads is pumped into the fractures to keep them from closing up once the pumping pressure is released. At such great depths and pressures, the fractures would slam shut without the proppant, defeating the purpose.

If the combination of these techniques is successful, the result is an oil or gas well that can basically print money.

What has followed in the region since then has been a mad rush to mine "black gold"—especially when oil was trading above $100 per barrel. According to a 2013 estimate from the U.S. Geological Survey, the Bakken could contain 7.4 billion barrels of undiscovered, technically recoverable oil.

Those figures are nearly double the estimates from 2008, and most energy experts now agree that the "official" figure likely understates the region's full potential.

Today, North Dakota is pumping about 1.1 million barrels of crude per day—equal to an annual production figure of about 432 million barrels. That's more than six times the 79.7 million barrels produced in 2009.

Covering over 200,000 square miles of land, there are 10,439 producing wells in North Dakota today, up from just 891 active wells in 2009. In fact, experts now believe the Bakken will be producing energy for the next 100 years.

♖

THE COMBINED TECHNOLOGIES that made all of this possible are now being used in other fields all across the country.

And after 40 years of empty promises, the prospect of U.S. energy independence has become a reality. What started in earnest in the Bakken has set off ripples around the world.

Remember Peak Oil? It's dead and buried. Instead of scarcity, the world has arrived at a very different tipping point.

The vast new fields and the new drilling techniques developed in the U.S. have created a "supply shock" that is turning the Great Game on its head. In geopolitical terms, it represents a true paradigm shift—the end of an established order.

It's the energy equivalent of the Berlin Wall coming down, and it's setting off a chain reaction all over the world. For the U.S., the new-found oil boom represents a dramatic reversal of fortune.

And even Saudi Arabia's November 2014 decision to have OPEC defend market share and drive oil prices down didn't stop the march of U.S. shale.

After falling for 30 years, U.S. oil production has skyrocketed since 2010. Again, the Saudi-led OPEC push to drive down oil prices barely made a dent.

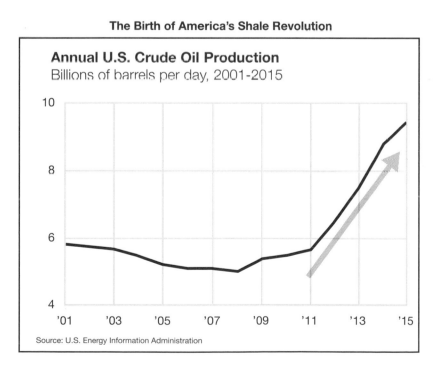

The Birth of America's Shale Revolution

Annual U.S. Crude Oil Production
Billions of barrels per day, 2001-2015

Source: U.S. Energy Information Administration

Today, the Bakken is being eclipsed by two even more productive shale formations in Texas: the Eagle Ford Shale and the Permian Basin.

Often referred to as the "Texas Bakken," the Eagle Ford Shale extends across Texas from the Mexican border up into East Texas, encompassing an area roughly 50 miles wide and 400 miles long with an average thickness of 250 feet.

According to preliminary data released by the Texas Railroad Commission, the nine fields that make up the majority of Eagle Ford yielded 764,438 barrels of crude on a single day in January 2014.

Meanwhile, the Permian Basin is roughly 250 miles wide and 300 miles long, and is located in western Texas and southeastern New Mexico. This basin alone is producing almost 2 million barrels of oil per day.

In fact, in March 2014, Texas oil production reached its highest level since 1980. In all, the Lone Star State pumped more than 77.2 million barrels of crude for the month, up 22.4% from the same time period in 2013—a number that itself has been beaten every year since.

To put it into perspective, all you need to do is look at the chart below. The surge in Texas crude has been exponential . . .

The Oil Renaissance in The Lone Star State

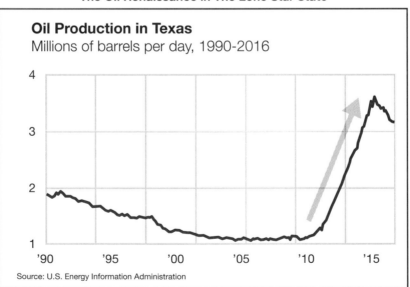

Oil Production in Texas
Millions of barrels per day, 1990-2016

Source: U.S. Energy Information Administration

As of December 2016, Texas controlled a staggering 49.84% of the oil and natural gas drilling rigs in operation today across the U.S. Globally, Texas manages to command a 34% share.

Texas currently produces more than 3.4 million barrels of oil per day, putting it ahead of Venezuela, Kuwait, Mexico and the United Arab Emirates, becoming the equivalent of the eighth largest oil-producing "nation" in the world.

In all, U.S. "tight-oil" production averaged 4.9 million BPD in 2015, enough to lift total U.S. output to 9.4 million BPD in 2015, accounting for more than 10% of world production. And in March 2014, almost two-thirds of the tight-oil output came from the Eagle Ford and the Bakken shale in North Dakota and Montana.

But it's not just about Texas and North Dakota. There's a massive amount of oil buried in formations all across the country. At 15 billion recoverable barrels, the Monterey Shale could be bigger than the Bakken and Eagle Ford combined, according to a new report prepared for the EIA.

That's in addition to:

1. **The Green River formation in Wyoming with the potential for 800 billion barrels of oil.**
2. **The Tuscaloosa Marine Shale, in Louisiana and Mississippi, with nearly 7 billion barrels of recoverable oil.**
3. **The Wolfcamp shale formation in Texas, which could hold 20 billion barrels of recoverable reserves.**
4. **And the New Albany shale basin in Illinois, which is estimated to have 300 billion barrels of oil. That's more than twice the amount of recoverable oil in Iraq.**

So the truth is we are still in the *very* early stages of the shale oil boom.

According to the Energy Information Administration (EIA), U.S. crude oil production should rise from 9.4 million BPD in 2015 to about 11.5 million BPD in 2030.

These numbers are so large, predictions that U.S. oil supply would peak are now a distant memory. As a result, the U.S. will need much less in the way of imports.

In fact, U.S. oil imports peaked at 60% in 2005 and fell below 25% in 2015, the lowest since 1970.

This flood of new crude has created what the International Energy Agency is now calling a "supply shock"—as in too much oil.

According to the Paris-based agency, this new abundance of shale oil will be "as transformative to the market over the next five years as was the rise of Chinese demand over the last 15."

As a Great Game element, that spells big trouble for the members of the old order—namely OPEC and Russia.

According to the IEA, non-OPEC supplies are expected to grow by 6 million BPD to 59.3 million BPD in 2018. About 65% of the growth will come from North American light, tight-oil and Canadian oil sands production.

"North America has set off a supply shock that is sending ripples throughout the world," according to then-IEA Executive Director, Maria van der Hoeven.

This rapid increase in North American oil production is expected to outrun the growth in global demand during the next few years, which is forecast to grow at about 1.4 million BPD annually—at least in the near term. It implies the demand for OPEC oil exports during the next five years is likely to be much weaker than had been expected—and as OPEC's late-2016 decision to cut production shows.

"The technology that unlocked the bonanza in places like North Dakota can and will be applied elsewhere," says van der Hoeven, "potentially leading to a broad reassessment of reserves. But as companies rethink their strategies, and as emerging economies become the leading players in the refining and demand sectors, not everyone will be a winner."

And there's another "supply shock" element the IEA is completely missing.

While the IEA is focused primarily on U.S. on-shore shale-oil production, there also the simultaneous revolution in off-shore technology that is enabling the discovery and development of huge fields in the Gulf of Mexico.

Those technologies include improved seismic imaging, the computational power to process the images, and the still-limited application of new stimulation techniques in off-shore fields.

♖

IN SHORT, THE U.S.-led on-shore revolution is now leading to a second wave off-shore, adding even more potential growth to the non-OPEC supply.

These "supply shock" changes will transform the way the oil market works, causing oil companies to overhaul their global investment strategies, reshaping the way oil is transported, stored and refined—not to mention how the Great Game is played.

That doesn't even consider the impact of future U.S. shale gas production. As with oil, it's a game changer in every sense of the often overused phrase. But in this case, it really fits.

A recent Rice University study projects that U.S. shale gas production will more than quadruple by 2040 from 2010 levels of more than 10 billion cubic feet per day, reaching more than 50% of total U.S. natural gas production by the 2030s.

It's led by a sleeping giant spanning a vast area of the Northeast called the Marcellus Shale.

No less than three recent studies—one from the U.S. Energy Information Administration, one from *Morningstar,* and one from *Moody's Investor Service*—have concluded that over the next few years, the Marcellus shale gas fields will be the most productive shale gas play in the U.S.

"Technological advancements since the early 2000s have allowed U.S. natural gas producers to reshape the industry largely through the development of the Marcellus," wrote *Moody's* analyst Michael Sabella in a March 3 report. "The Marcellus has emerged as one of the most profitable regions in the U.S. for producing natural gas, so even if prices return to the weak levels of 2012, [natural gas stocks] will be rewarded."

And *Morningstar* predicted that the Marcellus will account for one-quarter of all U.S. natural gas production, with production increasing from 14 billion cubic feet per day to 20 billion.

"The growth of the Marcellus over the next several years is likely to be nothing short of astounding," said the *Morningstar* report, which attributed the rapid growth to efficiency improvements.

"For a variety of reasons—including the high initial production rates and relatively shallow declines of wells, the ongoing application of new technologies, and a continued focus on more productive areas of the play—we don't believe Marcellus natural gas production will reverse course anytime soon," the *Morningstar* report says.

According to the EIA report, Marcellus shale gas production even now has grown to the point where, if it were its own country, it would rank third behind Russia and the rest of the U.S.

With the Marcellus estimated to have between 30 and 75 years' worth of natural gas reserves, companies operating there stand to make decades worth of profits.

There's also the Barnett basin in Texas. It still contains 44 trillion cubic feet of gas, which is more than THREE-times what it has been produced so far. There are also the Fayetteville shale in Arkansas, the Haynesville shale in Louisiana, and the Utica shale in Ohio and New York, just to name a few.

To my knowledge there isn't a single oil or gas basin in America that is even close to being depleted.

But it's not just a local story. Not by a long shot. After years of explosive growth in the U.S. and Canada, the shale oil and gas craze is starting to go global.

Now make no mistake, a head start in a business this critical is huge. But the rest of the world is catching up—and fast.

The first markets may have been U.S. and Canadian, but the biggest shale oil and gas markets are actually abroad. They include massive finds in areas you wouldn't ordinarily think of.

But to understand just how much bigger this "supply shock" is about to become, and the effect it will have on the Great Game in the future, you need to see this map.

The Global Shale Revolution

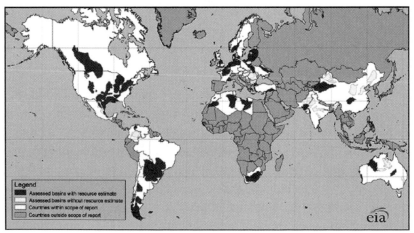

It's a picture that paints a thousand words . . .

This well-known map has a few interesting wrinkles to it. First, much of the world (shown here in grey) is not even included in the survey.

The areas outside the study include Russia and most of the Middle East. And we already know there are considerable shale formations in each, leading to the conclusion that much of the world's available shale gas is not even in the survey.

Second, preliminary calculations have concluded that the top four reserves of shale gas globally are found in China, the U.S., Argentina, and Mexico.

Subsequent EIA calculations have since provided a better indication of what these basins actually look like, leading to this version put together by *Reuters*.

Global Shale Gas Basins, Top Reserve Holders

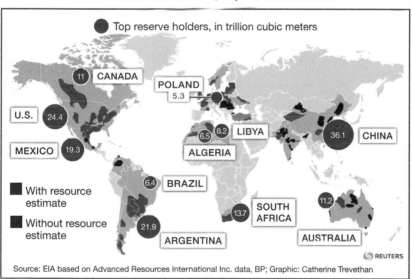

Source: EIA based on Advanced Resources International Inc. data, BP; Graphic: Catherine Trevethan

So as you can see, there are significant shale gas resources to be found in numerous places *outside* of North America.

And nearly every one of them will require large doses of American ingenuity, giving the U.S. a big technological inroad into nearly every critical corner of the globe.

What started as just an idea, has given the U.S. a valuable upper hand. It includes a brand-new export market that didn't even exist in 2007 . . .

The New American Dawn

THE SUDDEN DEVELOPMENT of significant unconventional gas reserves has put the United States in a veritable cat bird's seat. This "super shift" is so profound, it promises to help create a new American dawn.

With enough natural gas to meet current consumption levels for nearly 100 years, America's position on the Great Game board has been strengthened in ways that nobody thought was possible just seven years ago.

This growing largess has changed everything we used to think about natural gas, affecting energy markets both here at home and abroad.

Today, we're waking up to a "gas-driven" world.

This stunning transformation is made up of four rapidly expanding components. Three of them are local, but the last has the greatest Great Game implications of them all.

First, natural gas is replacing oil as a feeder stock for petrochemicals. It includes everything from ingredients used in the production of plastics to fertilizers and widely used chemicals. This is simply replacing oil products like naphtha. This transition has been underway for a while now.

In fact, the intense competition over where to locate the new multi-billion dollar cracker installations needed for this process is a testament to the upward curve in petrochemicals as a demand-side absorber of gas supply.

Second, we continue to see a move toward liquefied natural gas (LNG) and compressed natural gas (CNG) as a vehicle fuel. This transition will take the longest to develop. It's already here for top-range trucks and mass transit, where LNG and compressed natural gas (CNG) are already seeing a rapid increase in truck and bus fleet retrofits.

It's the average passenger vehicle where this transition has been the slowest. Much like the advent of hybrids, the cost of these engines is still not competitive. But that will also eventually come to pass.

However, it's the last two categories that are going to be the biggest drivers of change.

One involves the move from coal to gas for the production of electricity. This shift is now well underway. And while coal still has a place in the overall energy balance, its days of controlling the domestic power sector are long gone.

I regularly analyze and revise these conversion figures for one simple reason: They tell us something truly remarkable.

By 2020, it is estimated that the U.S. will be replacing 90 gigawatts (GW) of capacity, virtually all of that coal-fueled. Most of this is simply due to facility age. Yet there will likely be additions to the total coming from new Environmental Protection Agency (EPA) regulations.

Forget, for a moment, about the introduction of stricter carbon emission standards. The phase-in of non-carbon standards is having an immediate impact, involving the cutting of mercury, sulfurous, and nitrous oxide emissions. These alone may well add another 20 to 30 GW to the capacity transition.

Now here's the point: My initial read in the early 2010s was a 1 billion cubic foot per day increase in gas needs for each 10 GW of electricity transitioned. That estimate turned out to be low. The current level is now 1.2 billion.

In addition, the move from coal to gas is happening faster than I had anticipated. Of the new plants on the drawing board and at the FEED (front end engineering and design) stage, there are no new coal-fueled or even coal/gas co-fueled plants of any appreciable size planned.

But it's the last element that is the biggest of the all, especially in geopolitical terms.

It's the advent of LNG exports from the U.S. This movement is so strong and unstoppable, it has the power to change the world.

It's the result of one of the biggest reversals of fortune I have ever witnessed.

You see, in 2005, everyone agreed (myself included) that the U.S. would be using liquefied natural gas (LNG) *imports* to meet 15% of its gas needs by 2020.

Now, even Russia's gas behemoth Gazprom acknowledges that the U.S. could be *providing* between 8% and 12% of all worldwide LNG exports in 2020. That's up from almost zero LNG exports today.

In the larger picture, that gives the U.S. a powerful new piece on the board.

As a result, America is scrambling to retool LNG import facilities for exports and to build new LNG export facilities, with the business of Japan, China, South Korea, the European Union and others at stake.

So why is LNG such a game-changer?

It's simple. LNG is a major transition because it allows you to move natural gas anywhere in the world. LNG is simply natural gas that is cooled to -260° Fahrenheit until it becomes a liquid. This process reduces its volume by about 600 times—similar to reducing the volume of a beach ball to the volume of a ping-pong ball.

In this state, it can now be shipped anywhere in the world you can get a train, ship, or truck.

Once delivered to its destination, the LNG is warmed back up into its original gaseous state so that it can be used in the traditional manner, by sending it through pipelines for distribution to homes and businesses.

This transformation means the practical use of natural gas is *no longer limited* to those few areas around the globe that are adjacent to pipelines. Freed from these limitations, natural gas is no longer simply a localized energy source.

As a liquid, it becomes a much more valuable **global** commodity.

All the LNG export boom needs now is something of a push forward to get the ball rolling. Fortunately, that's exactly what's about to happen with the arrival of two new catalysts.

The first catalyst is export approvals from Uncle Sam. Right now, there's a mad rush to get LNG export licenses approved.

As of today, there are at least 65 current or proposed terminal projects that have filed applications to export LNG.

The seventh to receive approval was Jordan Cove Energy Project LP in March 2014. The company was granted conditional authorization to export liquefied domestic natural gas to countries that are not parties to a free trade agreement (FTA) with the U.S. from the Jordan Cove LNG Terminal in Coos Bay, OR.

♜

BUT THE UNQUESTIONED leader in this game is Cheniere Energy. And more than any other company, this one is set up to positively explode now that the Panama Canal expansion is complete, since it is opening up the lucrative Asian markets almost overnight.

Cheniere already has five huge multi-billion dollar, 20-year export contracts with some of the top players in the LNG market and blanket permission from the U.S. Department of Energy to begin LNG exports.

Long-term contracts with BG Group plc, Total SA, Korea Gas Corp., India's GAIL Ltd. Spain's Gas Natural Fenosa and the U.K.'s Centrica plc should translate into $2.6 billion a year in revenue once Sabine Pass becomes fully operational.

To meet this growing demand, Cheniere is developing a liquefaction project adjacent to the Sabine Pass LNG terminal for up to six LNG trains with aggregate capacity of approximately 27 million tons per year (mt/y).

Sabine Pass was the first—and until recently, the only—project allowed to export LNG to countries without a free trade agreement with the United States.

The project sits on the Sabine Pass deep-water shipping channel on the Louisiana side of the border with Texas. It has access to all the major shale gas basins including the Marcellus, Utica, Eagle Ford, Barnett, and Haynesville basins.

As this market heats up, you can be sure many more approvals will follow.

Cumulatively, the approved licenses now mean as much as 51.33 billion cubic feet of American natural gas could be sent each day to non-free-trade partners. That would move the U.S. into "superpower" territory, far exceeding Qatar's 10.3 billion cubic feet of daily natural gas export capacity.

The second catalyst has to do with the widening of the Panama Canal which finished in 2016, doubling the canal's capacity.

This $5.25 billion project means the canal will now be able to admit the "New Panamax" sized super-tankers that are LNG-rated. These double-hull tankers are huge, highly specialized, and very expensive to operate.

That will enable U.S. gulf-based LNG export terminals to profitably service the booming Asian market—where LNG demand is growing the fastest.

The First Steps in a Massive New Export Market

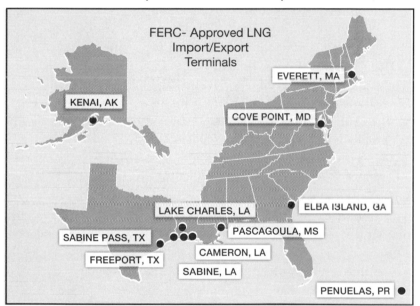

In fact, the improved canal will cut America's current LNG shipping routes to Asia by 8,500 miles each way.

The bottom line of this growing boom is simple: Liquefied natural gas is going to change the global energy game—and the U.S. will soon be at the head of the LNG pack.

But those are not the only developments that are going to boost the LNG export market. Over the next 12 months, a monumental change in pricing structure promises to revolutionize the way natural gas is traded.

In fact, growing LNG exports are already altering delivery expectations, forcing conventional long-term pipeline contracts to be revised.

Rising LNG volumes undermine the conventional contract terms—especially in regions previously serviced by pipeline imports only.

Here's why . . .

In places like Western Europe, LNG is now providing spot markets to cut import prices. The availability of sufficient guaranteed LNG import volume also allows for the creation of a delivery hub to compete with long-term pipeline contract pricing.

These pipeline contracts usually extend for 20 years and have a "take-or-pay" provision requiring that a minimum percentage of the contracted volume be taken each month or the user pays for it anyway.

What's more, these contract prices are determined by a basket of crude oil and oil product prices. This last aspect creates major problems for importers when the price of crude oil is rising.

That's why establishing an LNG receiving hub surrounding a sufficiently large import terminal, like the Rotterdam Gate facility, will almost always guarantee spot pricing lower than pipeline contracts.

While this is great news for European end users, it creates significant problems for major exporters such as Gazprom.

As this American-anchored trading model expands, it promises to revolutionize certain long-standing relationships, putting the U.S. LNG market fully into motion.

Of course, evening out supply to meet demand within such a pricing environment would seem to require massive additional consignments of LNG.

And that is exactly what is rushing onto the scene.

Mitsubishi Corp. has provided a dramatic example of just how fast this trade is increasing. The figures are in million tons per year (mt/y).

According to Mitsubishi, a big LNG player, the industry is set to grow 56% by 2020. And whether as an exporter or importer, everybody is getting into the act.

Combining current export and import terminals with those approved and under construction, my own estimates suggest almost 200 terminals will be online before the end of the decade, having an aggregate export capacity of 508.4 mt/y and an import total in excess of almost 765 mt/y.

The excess capacity above and beyond the Mitsubishi figures (346 mt/y) can only lead me to one conclusion: *the global trading volume will be ramping up even more.*

One reason is the rapidly expanding Asian demand. The Asian natural gas market (even excluding OECD countries in the reagion) is the fastest growing market and is expected to become the second largest gas market in 2030 and the largest in 2040.

Projected LNG Demand Worldwide

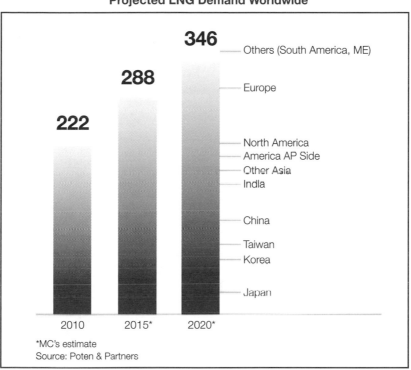

And aside from Japan, the Republic of Korea, and Chinese Taipei, importing LNG is a relatively new phenomenon. India started in 2005, China in 2006, Thailand in 2011, and Indonesia and Malaysia in 2012. And more Asian countries are expected to become LNG importers this decade.

Here's why.

In Asia, LNG is widely perceived as being decisive in moving its energy sector from a heavy dependence upon the region's inferior coal reserves. Not surprisingly, this move is being led by China.

Driven by its massive economic expansion, natural gas consumption has increased more than five-fold in China since 2000.

Asia-Pacific Natural Gas Imports/Exports, 2012-2040

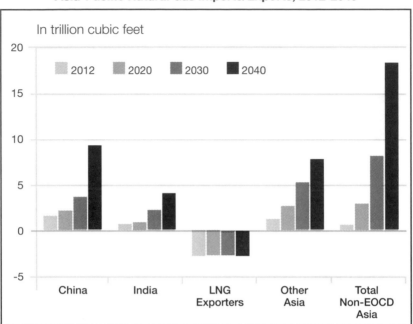

In fact, China continues to turn more to natural gas as a solution to the country's air pollution problem. The 12th Five-Year Plan to "gasify" the Chinese economy calls for the gas share of the energy mix to rise from 4% in 2010 to 8% by 2015, with a longer-term goal of a 10% share by 2020.

And beyond 2020, China's potential gas demand will be huge, considering that China's coal market is seven times larger than the total global LNG market.

As you might expect, China is moving quickly.

China first began importing LNG in 2006, but by the end of 2012 it had six LNG import terminals in operation. The total capacity of these terminals is 18.8 million tons of LNG.

By the end of 2014, China had another six LNG import terminals operational with another two under construction. Added capacity is expected to be about an extra 28.8 million tons. In addition, its first floating LNG terminal is now operational.

It's all part of larger movement worldwide to add diversity to the energy mix, diminishing the need to rely on supplies that are considerably more volatile and unreliable. And it's largely being driven by U.S. largess.

In fact, a recent study by the Baker Institute of Public Policy at Rice University concluded that increased shale gas production in the U.S. and Canada could help prevent Russia and Persian Gulf countries from dictating higher prices for the gas they export to European countries

As a Great Game strategy, it's an opportunity to isolate Iran and undermine Russian energy dominance, while creating broad benefits to the U.S. economy.

As a December 2012 Senate Foreign Relations Committee report found, NATO allies in Central Europe and Turkey would experience particularly potent national security gains from U.S. LNG trade as they seek to reorient their supplies away from both Russia and Iran.

Although initial volumes of U.S. natural gas sent overseas are likely to be small, they will go far to empower allies to stand up to energy coercion.

In fact, U.S. natural gas production is already affecting the geopolitics of energy. North African and Middle Eastern LNG, once scheduled for export to the U.S., has been diverted to European and other markets, providing alternatives to Russian gas while offering better pricing.

With U.S. natural gas prices now one-third to one-fifth of those in Europe and Asia, the U.S. can certainly expect a line of willing customers eager to tap into its reliable supply.

As it stands, U.S. LNG exports alone are projected to top $30 billion in revenues a year and stimulate $47 billion in domestic economic activity by 2020.

The other side of the coin is that those same domestic energy supplies are going to have a major impact on global trade.

According to a recent study by the Boston Consulting Group (BCG), "cheap" domestic energy could result in the U.S. taking between $70 and $115 billion in annual exports from other countries by the end of this decade.

This will provide significant economic advantages to America as this new era is ushered in.

Now I hasten to add upfront, the "cheap" energy referred to in the study is a relative matter. This is not the knee-jerk assumption of some that, if we have all of this shale gas and tight oil sitting around, that is bound to result in lower domestic energy costs.

We may well be able to cut imports, but the truth is the overall price you pay at the pump or when heating your home is subject to other factors.

Rather, it's that the energy will be "cheap" relative to what it costs elsewhere in the world. And that is becoming the key in a major global shakeup.

In 2015, according to the BCG's report entitled, "Behind the American Export Surge," natural gas prices in the U.S. are projected to be 60%–70% lower, while electricity may be 40%–70% lower, than in Europe and Japan.

But the American advantage hardly ends there.

The study also notes a source not likely to be considered by most, at least initially. That is, until you factor in other elements contributing to this energy advantage.

BCG points out that lower labor costs will also be important sources of a competitive advantage for manufacturing in the U.S. Adjusted for productivity, America's labor costs for many products are estimated to be 15%–35% lower than those of Western Europe and Japan within two years.

In addition, America will have a manufacturing cost advantage in machinery of roughly 7% over Japan, 14% over Germany and France, and 15% over Italy. But labor costs will be the big differentiator, BCG said.

That is a major shift in a very short period of time.

As *Gas Business Briefing* has reported, only a decade ago, average productivity-adjusted American factory labor costs were around 17% lower than in Europe, and only 3% lower than in Japan.

Here, the rise of domestic energy has been a major catalyst in a remarkable change.

♜

BEGINNING IN THE 1960s, all manner of manufacturing moved from high-cost to low-cost countries. Then, the emergence of competitors to U.S. factory dominance resulted from this transition.

However, one senior author of the BCG report concludes that, "Now, as the economics of global manufacturing changes, the pendulum is finally starting to swing back. In the years ahead, it could be America's turn to be on the receiving end of production shifts, as more companies use the U.S. as a low-cost export platform."

A range of economic sectors are identified as likely to benefit from this change, making the U.S. particularly well positioned to increase exports.

In the report, BCG lists seven specific industries in which American exports will be rising at the expense of competing nations. They include: chemicals, machinery, transportation equipment, oil and coal products, computer and electronic products, electrical equipment and appliances, and primary metals.

Of great interest is the BCG observation that these seven sectors account in the aggregate for about 75% of total global exports. In turn, employment gains would come directly through added factory work and indirectly through supporting services, such as construction, transportation, and retail, the report concludes.

But the industrial shakeup that is coming because of the energy advantage will be multifaceted.

Some companies will increasingly use the U.S. as a low-cost export base for the rest of the world, while others will use American production to replace imports. Throughout, both American and foreign companies will be relocating the manufacturing of products sold in the U.S. that otherwise would have been made offshore.

"It will take several more years for the full impact of improved U.S. competitiveness to translate into significantly more jobs and higher industrial output," said Michael Zinser, a BCG partner who leads the firm's manufacturing practice in the Americas and a report co-author.

Yet Zinser adds, "We already are seeing early evidence. Foreign companies such as Toyota, Airbus, Yamaha, Siemens, and Rolls-Royce are starting to move more production to the U.S. for export around the world."

For example, by 2015, the U.S. was projected to take $7–12 billion in chemical exports from Western Europe and Japan. Fundamental to such a transition is the relative cost advantage of domestically produced natural gas, a major feedstock for chemicals.

BCG points out that production costs in Germany, where the natural gas used in chemical manufacturing will be more than three-and-a-half times more expensive, were projected to be 29% higher than in the U.S. by 2015. Meanwhile, gas costs were expected to be 16% higher in China and as much as 28% higher in France.

As the energy component's comparative advantage kicks in, it will have positive results in wide export categories. As another example, BCG projected that by 2015, the U.S. will take $3–12 billion from Western Europe and Japan in exports of machinery, including everything from a construction and industrial machinery, to engines and air conditioners, the study says.

So the energy component has never been more important to the U.S. economy than it is going to be in the next decade.

And that American economic expansion that is going to result will give the U.S. Great Game advantages that will be substantial.

But that's not the only advantage the U.S. brings to the board. The other is a remarkable new technology.

12

The Great Game Wild Card

"DILIGENCE IS THE MOTHER
OF GOOD FORTUNE."
— BENJAMIN DISRAELI

♜

IN THE GREAT GAME, there's a possible wild card that only one player holds.

It has the potential to make one of the world's superpowers the winner in the Great Game. The result could be not only energy independence, but a transformation from being one of the world's biggest energy importers to becoming one of its major exporters.

This wild card is a technological breakthrough I've been following for some time. And although the technological wild card is held by the United States, the technology behind it began in a nondescript office building in the tiny neighborhood of Overhoeks in North Amsterdam.

Now I admit, the Netherlands is not what anyone would consider one of the world's oil heavyweights. Currently, this small country produces less oil in a given year than New Zealand, in itself hardly a major player.

But inside a heavily fortified five-story building on a small island on the edge of the Ij River, scientists made a discovery that could turn the oil industry, and by extension the entire energy industry, on its head.

More importantly, U.S. oil refiners have embraced this new technology, and are far ahead of the rest of the world.

The technology is called catalytic cracking or hydrocracking. It essentially turns 100 barrels of the cheapest crude oil and oil waste products available into 135 gallons of far more valuable diesel, jet and other fuels.

In essence, it uses sophisticated new technology to produce "free oil," and U.S. companies are the world leaders in applying it.

In fact, this technology turns the usual oil refining paradigm upside down.

Oil refineries that use conventional technology operate at 65–90% efficiency. If 100 gallons of light sweet crude, the highest quality unrefined oil, goes into the refinery, 65–90 gallons of gasoline, diesel fuel, jet fuel, kerosene and other oil derivatives are the result.

The remainder is primarily a thick sludge called residuum, which is typically considered waste. And it's environmentally unfriendly waste at that.

It was considered waste, that is, until scientists made a startling discovery—by processing the residuum with a mixture of hydrogen and chemical catalysts, the sludge could be converted into jet fuel, diesel, and gasoline.

In essence, it's like creating free oil. It would be the equivalent of taking banana peels and egg shells out of your trash, tossing them into a black box on your kitchen counter, and then opening that box to discover fresh eggs and perfectly ripe bananas.

The processing device, called a hydrocracker, not only boosts profits, but is good for the environment.

In fact, after performing a series of tests, the U.S. Department of Energy said that "free oil" technology was as good for the environment as it was for the refiners' bottom lines. By reclaiming the residuum, whose disposal poses serious environmental challenges, the DOE says the energy industry has turned oil into the equivalent of a renewable resource.

Because of the way residuum is processed, the "free oil" eliminates 1.57 million metric tons of CO_2 emissions each year, the equivalent of the combined amount of CO_2 generated by San Francisco, San Jose, and Sacramento, California.

According to the U.S. Environmental Protection Agency (EPA), it's also a "green energy" that is already responsible for over $37.5 billion in clean fuel savings.

Products Made from a Barrel of Crude Oil

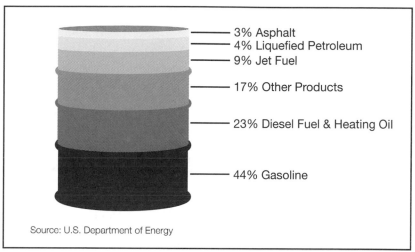

3% Asphalt
4% Liquefied Petroleum
9% Jet Fuel

17% Other Products

23% Diesel Fuel & Heating Oil

44% Gasoline

Source: U.S. Department of Energy

This green "free oil" technology can save Americans 19.154 trillion BTUs of energy a year.

That means it already produces enough energy savings—just in this country, just in these early stages—to power the entire state of Vermont, as well as 279,000 cars.

The trucking industry also predicts significant benefits from this breakthrough technology. The tractor-trailers that haul around all of our goods, as well as millions of industrial products and supplies, represent 16% of the energy consumed in America today. A recent report—prepared by executives from Sierra Pacific, PG&E, Berkley National Laboratory, and Dow Chemical—determine this "free oil" technology could reduce those trucks' energy consumption by 26%.

That adds up to 9.4 billion gallons of diesel fuel, and a savings of $37.5 billion every year. For companies that were previously weighing the benefits of retrofitting their trucks to run on alternative fuels, such as natural gas, eliminating the $35,000 per vehicle retrofit fee will result in additional savings.

The Organization for Economic Co-operation and Development (OECD), whose goal is to promote policies that will improve the economic and social well-being of people around the world, estimates that it will be 94% cheaper to cut greenhouse gasses using this technology, than with other renewable energy.

And those benefits can only increase as more U.S. refiners adopt this technology.

The technology couldn't have come at a better time.

Conventional refiners produce more gasoline than anything else from crude oil—approximately 50–60% of their output is gasoline, 25–30% is diesel and jet fuel, and the remainder is asphalt, other lubricants, and other petroleum products.

Hydrocracking also produces more low-sulfur fuels, such as diesel and jet fuel, than gasoline, just as the world demand for low sulfur fuels is skyrocketing. Ever-tightening federal regulations require that sulfur emissions be reduced, and hydrocracking can go a long way toward helping achieve those goals.

The increased output of low-sulfur fuel, in particular ultra-low sulfur diesel, (ULSD), also opens up new export possibilities for U.S. refiners and oil companies, since many other countries have even more stringent sulfur emissions standards than the U.S. Of course, following the 2015 Volkswagen diesel emmissions scandal, Europe is now moving away from using the fuel in cars. But industrial uses are expected to continue growing, and should make up any shortfall soon.

The result will be to flip the U.S. from a net oil importer to a net oil exporter, completely changing the landscape of the energy industry and drastically reducing the influence that OPEC nations, in particular the Middle East, have in the world. The growing worldwide market for oil will only accelerate the process—energy demand is expected to rise by 40% over the next 20 years—and in turn give the U. S. even greater influence in the world.

It's a remarkable new strategic move for an industry that saw four dozen U.S. refineries shut down in the 1990s.

The new technology won't completely change the U.S. import-export situation. Chances are the U.S. will import and export gasoline and other oil products simultaneously, with the Gulf Coast sending refined products overseas and the East Coast buying foreign supplies to satisfy regional demand. The reason: Existing pipelines and other oil transportation infrastructure cannot meet peak East Coast energy demands.

And the U.S. probably will still import more gasoline than it produces to satisfy domestic consumers during the peak summer demand season, according to Energy Security Analysts Inc. (ESAI) analyst John Galante.

Still, America's emergence as an energy exporter will be, according to the International Energy Association (IEA), "the straw that broke the camel's back" when it comes to the Middle East's power and influence in the Great Game.

There's another benefit to the technology, too.

The equipment can be smaller and lower profile than conventional oil refining equipment. This new technology can be housed in a distillation tower one-third the height of a conventional tower. Not only would this boost the businesses of smaller refiners, but the new technology can be added to existing refiners or constructed elsewhere with lower space requirements than conventional technology.

Refiners constantly monitor what the industry terms the "crack spread"—the difference in price between crude oil and various refined petroleum products. The crack spread helps refiners calculate the maximum potential profit from a given quantity of oil. By changing the percentages of gasoline, diesel, and other fuels that can be produced from crude oil, refiners have more ways to maximize their profits while meeting market demand.

For refiners, the good news gets even better. Hydrocracking can not only be used on residuum, but on other crude oil products as well. The oil industry characterizes crude oil, known as "feedstocks," as higher or lower quality, depending upon the amount of processing necessary and the output mixture. With hydrocracking, lower quality, cheaper feed stocks can be significantly more profitable than they are with conventional refining technology.

So without drilling another oil well, or floating another oil rig in the ocean, the U.S. can boost its oil reserves and production by 35%.

Other, related industries will benefit as well, such as the railroad, pipeline, shipping, and other companies that transport crude and refined oil and other petroleum products throughout North America and the world.

In an interesting twist, "free oil" technology will not vault the U.S. into the ranks of oil exporting countries, but return it to them. Thanks to the oil boom in Pennsylvania, the U.S. was the world's leading oil producer in 1870, and oil was the country's second biggest export after agricultural products.

At the time it was kerosene for lamps, not gasoline for automobiles, that was the prize. But the almost simultaneous invention of electric lights and the horseless carriage pushed the fledgling energy industry towards modern times.

"Free oil" technology won't remove energy from the Great Game, but it will become a U.S. power play with global implications.

Is the Great Game all about energy? Is it mostly about energy? Some would argue that the Great Game has several arenas, several playing fields, and energy is only one of them. Water is another.

But the end game could play out in an area that no one might have predicted. Just like energy and water, the conflict begins, and possibly ends, as a battle over natural resources.

However, this battle isn't about how technology can change the acquisition and use of these natural resources. It's about how technology *depends* upon them.

You see, the next great battle in the Great Game is likely to be over rare earths. Though completely misnamed, rare earths have the same geopolitical implications that energy does.

And, like oil, the U.S. was once a dominant player, then faded due to economic, environmental, and other factors.

The question now is whether or not the U.S. can regain its world dominance in this arena. In this case, the answer is far from clear.

13

America's Soft Underbelly

"THE MIDDLE EAST HAS OIL AND
CHINA HAS RARE EARTH"

— DENG XIAOPING, CHINESE COMMUNIST LEADER

♜

THE MINES WHERE iPhones are born—along with Toyota Priuses, wind turbines, lasers, stereo speakers, camera lenses, disk drives, night vision goggles, automotive catalytic converters, and many other indispensable elements of modern technology—may look like giant craters.

But they're really critical battlegrounds in the Great Game.

And just as the balance of power among the U.S., China, the Middle East, and other nations is continually shifting in the energy industry, the same thing is true about what the Japanese call "the seeds of technology" and the U.S. Department of Energy terms "technology metals."

You know them as rare earth metals.

What you may not know is that the 15–17 (depending upon how you classify them) elements classified as rare earths are neither rare nor earth. But, just as oil, natural gas, and coal are critical to modern life, rare earths are integral parts of modern technology.

An iPhone, for example, uses eight of them, and the U.S. Department of Energy designates five of them as critical to the U.S. in the short- and long-term. And, just as the dominant players in the energy industry have shifted, so have the nations that control rare earth elements, rare earth minerals, or simply rare earths.

Because rare earth elements are so important, they are as great a factor in the Great Game as oil or natural gas. And, like energy resources, they are a major factor in geopolitical maneuvering, disputes, and trade among the world's most powerful nations.

Scandium, Neodymium, Terbium, and the other elements that we call rare earths are considered "rare" because it is unusual to find them in their pure form, not because they're hard to come by.

Cerium, for example, is the 25th most common element in the world, about as common as copper. And there's more Lanthanum in the earth's crust than there is silver or lead.

Rare earths are essential elements used to produce a wide range of modern products. Neodymium is used to make magnets that are incredibly strong for their size. Those magnets make everything from wind turbines to oil drills possible. A Toyota Prius has ten pounds of Lanthanum in its batteries. When a battery is referred to as "nickel-metal hydride," the "metal" is Lanthanum. The result is a battery twice as efficient as the traditional lead-acid car battery.

Europium gives LED lights their white, bright color. Erbium "amplifies" the signal in fiber optics and lasers, making both much more efficient and effective.

The problem is in the environmental costs in mining and extracting them. Although technology has made extracting rare earths easier since the first one was discovered in 1787, many of the quarries where rare earths are mined are toxic messes.

The reason is simple: Rare earths make up, at most, 8% of the matter extracted from a rare earths mine. The remaining 92% is waste offering no commercial value, slightly radioactive, and loaded with toxic chemicals used in the extraction process.

The traditional method of processing this toxic stew is to pump the leftover 92% into what becomes a pond of radioactive waste, and try to keep it from spreading into nearby water sources. As the raw ore is crushed, heated, chemically washed, and separated, the tailings left behind are nothing short of an environmental nightmare.

What makes this extraction and processing so difficult is the fact that rare earths are often found together. So it requires a lot of chemistry and metallurgy to separate them from each other and purify them. Many of these mines also contain radioactive Thorium, which has to be handled separately. Recycling rare earths is also beyond difficult and rarely done, though Japan has begun some small-scale recycling projects.

Unlike oil and natural gas, rare earths are distributed around the globe. Because of the financial and environmental costs involved in extracting them, countries that were once large producers of these critical materials are, in many cases, out of the rare earths industry.

Until 1948, for example, most of the rare earths were sourced from placer sand deposits in Brazil and India. Production shifted to South Africa in the 1950s when large veins of Monazite were found. Then, when color television was invented, and rare earths were the materials needed to make color screens so colorful, production shifted to Mountain Pass, California, which was the world's leading producer of rare earths from the 1960s into the 1980s.

Then China entered the game.

Not surprisingly, it didn't take long for the Chinese to recognize the importance of rare earth elements. As Deng Xiaoping, the former leader of the Communist Party of China, noted back in 1992, "The Middle East has oil and China has rare earth." With that, China's power play for these minerals began.

Initially, China began extracting and separating rare earths as part of the iron-mining process in Inner Mongolia, dumping the tailings in huge man-made ponds. When nearby crops began to fail and illness rates rose, farmers and villagers quickly abandoned the area that then became known as the rare earth capital of the world. Though residents complained of everything from teeth falling out to high incidents of diabetes and cancer, the mining and processing continued.

With cheap labor and little concern for environmental safeguards, or even its own citizens, China was able to undercut U.S. prices and become the world leader in rare earths, just as the world market for these materials exploded.

The results were predictable: the costs of extracting and processing rare earths in the U.S., along with increasing awareness of the environmental hazards, caused U.S. production of rare earths to drop to zero. Meanwhile, China's share of global rare earths production, according to various sources, rose to between 85–95%.

Suddenly, technology companies had virtually only one source for these critical materials: China. And China capitalized on its power by

Rare-Earth Supply and Demand

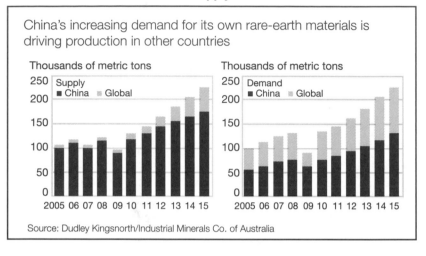

China's increasing demand for its own rare-earth materials is driving production in other countries

Source: Dudley Kingsnorth/Industrial Minerals Co. of Australia

lowering output and raising prices.

In 2011, China reduced its exports by 35%. When confronted by the U.S., Japan, and the European Union at a World Trade Organization meeting in 2012, China defended its drastic cuts in exports as a move to save the environment, and a long-running legal case began.

A diplomatic dispute between Japan and China over disputed territory in the South China Sea later led China to temporarily suspend shipments of rare earth elements to Japan—a move that caught the world's attention. A Chinese embargo temporarily halted all shipments of Chinese rare earths until world pressure forced—or perhaps, persuaded—the Chinese to lift the embargo.

As a result, prices skyrocketed by as much as 3,000% before dropping back to "only" 500% of the January 2008 price. In case after case, China has used the threat (or reality) of constrained supplies as a geopolitical weapon against Japan and other countries—although the Chinese have consistently denied that politics played a role in these decisions.

Given China's position of strength, it became obvious that the world, particularly the U.S., needed to find another resource for these critical elements. Formerly closed mines began formulating plans to reopen, as new mines were started in Malaysia and other areas.

That includes an effort by Molycorp Minerals to reopen the Mountain Pass mine in the Mojave Desert of California, about 60 miles south-west of Las Vegas, which closed in 2002. Meanwhile, Lynas Corporation, an Australian company, began developing the Mount Weld area in Western Australia, as well as facilities elsewhere.

But with financial, logistical and environmental considerations making the development process of a mine a 5–10 year process, current activities weren't sufficient to meet the growing demand for rare earths. What the U.S. needed was a breakthrough.

♜

IT OCCURRED IN a place few would have ever suspected—a war-torn country known as "the graveyard of empires." Not coincidently, it's a place with a prominent position in Mackinder's "Heartland."

Afghanistan.

Once a focal point of the Silk Road and an early participant as a buffer state between two former empires—British India and the Russian Empire—the war-torn country is sitting on nearly $1 trillion in untapped mineral deposits, the U.S. believes.

Vast stores of iron, copper, cobalt, gold, lithium and other materials, including rare earths, are believed to exist in rich veins, making it potentially one of the most important mining centers in the world.

The earliest estimates of these riches were based on Soviet field notes but for the most part these guesses were made sight unseen. It wasn't until U.S. geologists hiked through the "mineralized zone" and spotted large amounts of canary-yellow Bastnasite, the same mineral that harbors most of the world's rare earth reserves, that they knew they'd hit pay dirt.

According to the geologists, the amount of Bastnasite was unlike anything they'd ever seen before, making it an almost certain treasure trove of rare earths.

In fact, a Pentagon memo later called the country the "Saudi Arabia of lithium," a critical component of many batteries.

If correct, this mineral wealth would far outstrip Afghanistan's current economy, which is primarily based on opium and other narcotics, as well as a number of fruits and nuts. Unfortunately, an uncertain political future, a corrupt government, and ongoing U.S. involvement make the situation unstable and unpredictable.

Even still, the U.S. Geological Survey (USGS) believes that the rare earths in Afghanistan could supply the entire world's needs for at least

10 years, possibly much longer. And in a country with 35% unemployment, and a per-capita GDP of approximately $1,100, there's little question that a robust mining industry would be welcome.

Because geologists have only been able to survey the least dangerous areas of the country, and then only under the watchful eyes of heavily armed U.S. soldiers, no one is sure how much in the way of mineral riches lies beneath the country. It would almost certainly be one of the world's largest producers of rare earths, and USGS officials believe the early estimates are likely to be conservative.

Yet beyond the current war and regional conflicts between warlords, developing the country's vast mineral deposits presents other difficulties.

For one thing, much of the needed infrastructure, including transportation, power and communications networks, is far from adequate. Building that infrastructure, and then bringing in the experts and equipment needed to begin development, would be an expensive, daunting task.

The bigger question is who would do it. The U.S. government? U.S. firms? The Afghani government, possibly in partnership with other nations or outside firms?

The Chinese, of course, have the financial and technological resources, as well as the desire, to develop the country's rare earth elements. The U.S., Japan, Russia, and the E.U. do as well.

In the meantime, the fledgling Afghanistan Ministry of Mines has begun formulating plans, while members of the International Security Assistance Force (ISAF), which consists of two-thirds U.S. forces, is heading for the exits after more than a decade of war and nation building.

But none needs them more so than the U.S. Currently, according to the U.S. Geological Survey, close to 60% of all rare earth elements used in U.S. manufacturing is imported—down from 100% in 2011, but still very high.

And the Congressional Research Service reports, "The concentration of production of rare earth elements (REEs) outside the United States raises the important issue of supply vulnerability. REEs are used for new energy technologies and national security applications. Two key questions of interest to Congress are: (1) Is the United States vulnerable to supply disruptions of REEs? (2) Are these elements essential to U.S. national security and economic well-being?"

The answer, according to the CRS, which has provided policy and legal analysis to committees and members of both the House and Senate for nearly a century, is definitive:

"Rare earths are critical to both U.S. national security and the economy, and the U.S., because almost all of its rare earth supplies comes from abroad, is vulnerable to price and supply fluctuations."

That makes the extraction, processing, and distribution of rare earths as critical as oil, gas, and other energy resources in the Great Game.

And, as in the energy industry, the geopolitical outcome on this playing field is far from clear.

But those worries are nothing compared to what happening in England. Once one of the biggest drivers of the original Great Game, the British Empire has certainly seen better days.

14

It's Midnight in London

I N THE LATE 19th and early 20th centuries, the sun literally never set on the British Empire. With British imperial power spanning the globe, it was always daylight somewhere among the UK's colonies and territories.

But since World War I, the light has been fading on the British Empire, and on the day that former Prime Minister Margaret Thatcher died—April 8, 2013—London came within hours of a massive blackout caused by energy shortages.

Britain's Queen in the Great Game, the vast oil and gas reserves of the North Sea, almost became its undoing.

Under Thatcher, the North Sea's oil and gas powered the British economy, putting billions of pounds into the country's coffers and allowing it to avoid much of the disruption caused by the oil embargoes of the 1970s.

While others scrambled for oil and natural gas, the UK was complacent, with huge reserves of oil and natural gas in the North Sea providing both energy independence *and* a false sense of security. For England, the world's energy troubles seemed far away.

But by the new millennium, the North Sea, which once represented

The North Sea: A Disappearing Giant

about 90% of the entire UK's energy reserves, was running out. Experts estimated that the country's reserves were down to a two-day supply, a razor-thin margin. Homes and businesses braced for massive blackouts as the power plants, which generated electricity from natural gas (at the time about 35% of England's electricity), prepared to shut down.

It was only an emergency shipment of two ships carrying liquefied natural gas from Qatar, the *Mehaines* and the *Zarga*, that averted disaster. The media breathlessly reported on the ships' progress, while British citizens watched and prayed.

A few years back, British Gas, the country's biggest energy supplier, warned that North Sea natural gas supplies are running out, and the UK's Office of Gas and Electricity Markets estimated that the region's natural gas wells will be done by the winter of 2015.

That didn't happen, but the "reserve margin of generation," the industry term for reliable spare capacity in the system, is set to fall from its current 14% to just over 4%, a tight margin with no room for any disruptions. Even a prolonged cold snap could wipe out that reserve.

The other issue is storage capacity. Lulled into a false sense of security by its North Sea reserves, the British can only store approximately a fortnight's worth of natural gas.

In comparison, Germany's stores would last 10 weeks. The result is the UK is more affected by supply fluctuations and price changes than many other countries, with little in the way of stored reserves to cushion the impact.

That leaves England with no easy energy alternatives: currently coal, nuclear, and renewable energy resources are only capable of supplying 60–70% of the country's energy needs.

And that percentage is set to fall. The European Union's Combustion Plants Directive of 2001 required old plants that were unable to meet strict new emission standards to close by 2015, or after a maximum of 20,000 hours of further operation.

Those regulations have already forced the closure of plants that provided approximately 10% of England's energy capacity, with more closures planned by 2015. In the aftermath of the worldwide banking crisis, financing for new plants has dried up, even when regulatory hurdles have been overcome.

Because three-quarters of all UK generating capacity is now owned by foreigners, the financial calculations for new plants are driven purely by dollars and cents (or pounds and shillings), not patriotism. Government incentives have, so far, been insufficient to spur large scale power plant construction. The only exception is the Hinkley Point C nuclear power station, which is years behind and is now estimated to cost Brititsh consumers four times as much as originally expected.

The solutions, if they come in time, will mostly come from thousands of miles away.

British energy company Centrica, the owner of British Gas, has contracts with both QatarGas and Russia's Gazprom Marketing & Trading Ltd. to buy LNG. The Qatar agreement, which extends a previous contract, runs through 2018 and could supply enough gas for 3 million homes (out of 26.4 million), or approximately 3 million metric tons. Gazprom is expected to supply about one-third less to the UK.

But the real growth in LNG imports is expected to come from the U.S. A 20-year deal with U.S. exporter Cheniere Energy, Inc will deliver LNG starting in 2018, and comes as British domestic gas production continues to decline. That gas, from U.S. shale deposits, comes from the fracking operations that have driven U.S. natural gas output to record highs; the same fracking operations that are currently mired in England's legal system.

♜

AS THE GREAT GAME unfolds, England is facing checkmate. Price hikes approaching double digits caused by dwindling reserves are already causing financial chaos. The once proud Empire is facing one of its greatest challenges of all-time.

Powerful political figures, such as Justin Welby, the Archbishop of Canterbury, have decried the price hikes. But all the jawboning in the world won't change the financial reality of dwindling supplies and growing demand.

For the short term, there is little question that British citizens and industry are facing an "energy poverty" situation that will have profound effects on the UK. To cut energy consumption by 30% or more (to match the loss of electricity from natural gas power plants) would reduce England to a de facto third-world country. Importing enough energy to compensate for the looming shortfall would bankrupt the country.

In the long term, the country really only has just one viable strategy: and it's not in the North Sea—it's right beneath their feet.

The British Geological Survey estimates there could be 1,300 trillion cubic feet of shale gas in the north of England. Three energy companies have been granted permission to test the Bowland shale gas reserves for the viability of fracking to retrieve that gas and any neighboring oil.

Experts believe that there are huge amounts of shale gas, at least 25 years' worth, waiting to be extracted from British land. British Prime Minister David Cameron is even more generous, estimating that Bowland Basin in the northwest could supply enough energy for 30 years. But there are significant environmental, financial and legal hurdles standing between England and the hope of an energy-filled future.

Environmentalists have staged protests against fracking and are continuing to pressure the government to drop the process from consideration. Opposition party leaders have decried the financial terms being discussed, claiming that current proposals for fracking don't do enough to support local economies, particularly rural areas.

Complicating the search for energy from shale is England's legal system.

The logistics of fracking typically require horizontal *and* vertical drilling, making it almost certain that any shale oil or gas extraction operation will not be confined to a well site, but include drilling under neighboring land. Those neighbors can use current anti-trespassing laws to prevent companies from drilling under their property.

Horizontal wells that stretch thousands of meters through narrow layers of rock will typically pass under several properties. If all of those property owners don't consent to drilling, the projects can be stopped.

In 2008, for example, Mohamed al-Fayed, the former owner of Harrods department store, successfully sued Star Energy U.K. Ltd. under laws of trespass for drilling under his estate in Surrey, England without seeking permission.

For landowners, there may not be a financial incentive to allow drilling. Unlike the U.S., landowners in England do not own the rights to the oil and gas, or certain other minerals, beneath the surface of their land. Those rights belong to the Crown or, in some cases, another third party. With no legal share in the profits, landowners often have little reason to grant drilling rights.

The result is a standoff. The country and its energy partners have a strong incentive to drill for the oil and natural gas trapped in shale, but anti-trespass laws prevent them from drilling under land they do not own. Landowners do not own the rights to the shale oil and gas under their feet, and thus are not guaranteed a share of the revenue if they allow drilling and fracking.

Meanwhile, the Church of England, citing laws that date back to the time of the Norman conquests, is claiming that it owns the mineral rights to over 500,000 acres, an area approximately the size of Sussex. In informing landowners of its intention to assert those rights, the church has said it has no plans to allow fracking at this time. But it has refused to rule out the future possibility of drilling for gas and oil.

To further complicate matters, the Queen has sent letters to over 2,600 landowners in Raunds and Irchester, asserting that the Crown holds the mineral rights to their land, and has for centuries.

Wells, such as an exploratory operation in Balcombe, a village south of London, by Cuadrilla Resources Ltd., have been mothballed while the legal process plays out.

Drilling supporters point out that underground rail, water, gas, telecommunications and electric development managed to clear landowner and trespass law hurdles, and fracking operations should be able to do the same.

Meanwhile, with imported energy causing energy costs to skyrocket in England, the country only has one choice: use energy more efficiently.

In the short term, the country is implementing new smart grid technology to keep the lights on. By using digital technology to allow every component in the country's electrical system, from generation to distribution to end users, officials believe they can cut costs, increase infrastructure security and more efficiently use scarce energy resources.

The Smart Grid Forum, which brings together industry, regulators and consumer groups, has outlined an ambitious plan that it believes will help both the country and the environment. Pilot projects, which have been used to test and develop smart grid technologies, have shown early promise.

As the technology is rolled out nationwide, forum members believe it will save British consumers £12 billion by 2050, as well as create 9,000 jobs.

Will it work? Will it be too little too late? Will the lights go out in London? Will crushing energy costs cause the economy to tank?

No one can say for sure. But the clock is ticking on the rapidly depleting energy reserves in the North Sea, and England's place in the Great Game is far from assured.

Meanwhile, events half a world away in Asia and the Middle East may trump any moves England makes. And at this point, the British citizenry remain pawns in the Great Game—quite a fall from grace.

15

An Alliance of Convenience

"THE SUPREME ART OF WAR IS TO SUBDUE THE ENEMY WITHOUT FIGHTING"

— SUN TZU

♜

ON THE FACE of it, China and Saudi Arabia would appear to have little in common.

The People's Republic of China is the world's most populous at 1.35 billion, Communist-ruled, and one of the world's fastest-growing economies since the introduction of economic reforms in 1978. They practice multiple religions—Confucianism, Buddhism, Taoism, Christianity and Muslim—though many adults practice no religion at all.

The Kingdom of Saudi Arabia, which was a largely nomadic region until the 1960s, is a 27 million-person monarchy, and virtually all are followers of Islam.

But they have one thing in common: an insatiable appetite for all things energy-related. China to fuel its continued expansion as a world power. Saudi Arabia to sustain its role as a dominant player in the world energy markets.

Where they come together is a place that few would have expected: the holy city of Mecca. One of the pillars of Islam, the city is the endpoint for a pilgrimage all Muslims are obliged to make at least once during their lifetime if they are able. The site gets almost two million visitors per year.

The reason is simple: the resource that propelled Saudi Arabia into major player status in the Great Game is running out. And Saudi Arabia hasn't yet positioned its pieces on the global chessboard for the future.

Currently, the importance of oil to the Saudis cannot be overstated. The country pockets $158 billion a year from exporting oil.

That represents:

- **85% of the nation's total export revenue.**
- **70% of the revenues for the government's budget.**
- **Well over 50% of the country's GDP.**

In short, the country is addicted to crude oil, and currently produces 12 million barrels of it a day. Saudi oil ministers claim to have one-fifteenth of the world's known oil reserves, but that cushion is fast disappearing.

Now the kingdom is facing increasing competition from the U.S.

According to the U.S. Energy Information Administration (EIA), the U.S. became the world's largest natural gas producer in 2010, and recently U.S. domestic oil production surpassed the amount of oil imported into the U.S.

The IEA predicts because of fracking, America will surpass Saudi Arabia and Russia as the world's largest oil producer in 2030.

Prince Alwaleed Bin Talal, a billionaire and a nephew of Saudi King Abdullah, has called the production of natural gas and shale oil in the U.S. and other countries, a threat to "any oil producing country in the world," especially his, and that Saudi Arabia "must do things to rectify the problem."

ONE OF THOSE things is a huge bet on an oil alternative, which the Saudis hope to use in conjunction with the Chinese to advance their stake in the Great Game. That bet has worldwide geopolitical implications.

What brings the Chinese and Arab worlds together in Mecca is a $109 billion project to turn Islam's holiest city into the first solar city in Saudi Arabia.

The Saudi Arabian government has formed the King Abdullah City for Atomic and Renewable Energy (KA-CARE) program to develop 41 gigawatts of solar capacity by 2040: 25 gigawatts in the form of solar thermal plants and 16 gigawatts from photovoltaic panels.

Currently, only about 3 megawatts of solar power plants are working in Saudi Arabia, a capacity that trails Egypt, Morocco, Tunisia, Algeria, and the United Arab Emirates (U.A.E.).

The Chinese, whose need for energy and relationships with energy providers is both enormous and growing, was an early partner with the Saudis. The Chinese firm ReneSola was recently awarded its first contract in the Middle East to provide 15 kilowatts of solar modules to be used in an off-grid power plant, which will also double up as a test bed for off-grid solutions.

The Saudi government also recently signed a nuclear cooperation agreement with China to build 16 nuclear reactors by 2031 at a cost of about $100 billion, further binding the geopolitical partnership. The kingdom plans to generate 20% of its electricity using nuclear energy.

In Mecca, according to Mayor Osama al-Bar, the city will need 385 gigawatt-hours of power each year, with 15–30% of it provided by solar energy operations.

Why the sudden interest in solar energy? So the country can preserve its dwindling oil reserves for export while powering its own growth.

Geographically, the kingdom is perfectly positioned to experiment with solar energy. The country gets more than twice the sunshine of anywhere in Europe, and researchers estimate that the Saudis receive between 4.5–7 kilowatts per square meter a day of solar radiation. In contrast, sunny Greece receives 1.7 kilowatts, according to the European Photovoltaic Industry Association.

Meanwhile, the U.S. is missing out on its share of the global solar photovoltaic revenue, estimated at $1 trillion for 2012–2018 alone because of its policies and political atmosphere, according to a new report from the Pew Charitable Trust lobbying group.

Numerous sources note that American photovoltaic installations have doubled in the last two years, but the additional capacity is still less than a third of that added by Germany or Italy. In 2011, China surpassed the U.S. in solar power generation for the first time.

As it becomes an energy partner with the most powerful energy exporter in the Middle East, China's influence on the region cannot be overstated. Saudi leaders see their alternative energy projects as catalysts that will spread throughout the Arab world, destabilizing an already unstable region.

Two Ships Passing in the Night

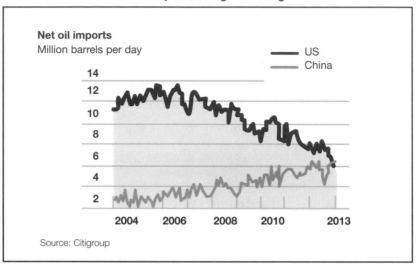

Net oil imports
Million barrels per day

Source: Citigroup

For the Chinese, becoming an integral part of the energy producing nations of the Middle East will increase the Communist country's influence over every country on the planet. For nations that depend upon the region for critical energy—virtually all Western nations—a spreading Chinese influence is a critical move in the Great Game being played out in the early years of the 21st century.

If the Chinese develop strength in the Middle East, it could lead to a Chinese stranglehold on critical energy resources—resources the U.S. cannot easily replace elsewhere.

As far back as 2013, the House Committee on Foreign Affairs held private hearings on the *Emerging Threat of Resource Wars* for this very reason, as China's economy, in the form of its GDP, has surged by 1,917% in two decades. China's "fuel" was initially cheap labor, but now the fuel is more literal.

Just as the U.S. triumphantly planted its flag on the moon to show its conquest of that planetary body, so is China planting its flag at critical energy and resource-rich regions in the Middle East and elsewhere in the world.

What does an alliance between Communists and a kingdom—between a Muslim country and one with no predominant religion—mean for the world? What does it mean when Saudi Arabia, the world's largest crude oil exporter, makes a major, $109 billion push to develop other energy sources?

It means the great geopolitical game practicality trumps ideology and dollars (or yuan and riyal).

It means that China is thinking five and even 10 moves ahead in the Great Game, while the U.S. loses a piece of its vast political edge.

And unfortunately, it means further destabilization and unpredictability in an already volatile region.

It also means that an unforeseen "wild card" becomes even more of a major player in the region.

That major player is Israel, where a big find in the Levant basin could transform Israel into a major world energy producer and change the geopolitical landscape in the Mediterranean.

16

A New Player at the Table

UNLIKE ITS MIDDLE East neighbors, the Israeli economy isn't built on oil. The country's economic stability is largely due to its advanced high-tech sector and agriculture rather than its production of raw materials.

Still, the Holy Land does produce some minerals and other substances that are useful for agriculture and industry.

But no one in the Great Game is concerned about Israel's potash (used to make fertilizer) or magnesium bromide (used in some medicines). Nations don't qualify for seats at the table for the Great Game with fertilizer.

What will advance Israel's pieces in the Great Game are the same strategic resources that have bought China, Russia, the U.S., and others seats at the table: energy.

In Israel's case, oil and natural gas could have huge geopolitical implications for the Middle East and the rest of the globe.

It could even spark a war: Lebanon and the Hezbollah vs. Israel—a war the U.S., and major players on both sides, could hardly ignore.

It is a myth that Israel has no oil. At the moment, Israel's oil industry is tiny though, producing barely over 1,000 barrels of oil per day.

After refining, that would be about the amount of gasoline needed to keep 30 American gas stations in business. For its Arab neighbors, Israel's annual oil production is equivalent to what many of them produce in a week, or in some cases a day.

But Israel's minor role in the energy industry is about to change.

Until recently, Israel's natural gas industry was also relatively small. But a few years ago, Israel and a small Texas company, Noble Energy Inc., collaborated to drill in the Tamar reservoir, 56 miles off the northern port city of Haifa in the Mediterranean Sea, close to a natural gas find made by Egypt.

After drilling five wells, they found what they were looking for—and the gas started flowing in 2013. Today, 40% of Israel's electricity is generated by natural gas, and the country is well on its way to energy independence.

That natural gas alone, added 1% to Israel's GDP in 2013, with much more to come.

But supplying its own needs isn't what will change the geopolitical stakes for Israel.

Nearby, exploratory drilling uncovered what experts called one of the largest offshore gas finds in a decade, in the area named the Levant or Levantine Basin. Israel claimed all rights to this massive "super-giant" gas field, declaring it an Exclusive Economic Zone (EEZ).

The basin, named after the Biblical sea monster (Leviathan), is estimated by Noble Energy to contain 16 trillion cubic feet of gas, making it the world's biggest deep-water gas find in a decade.

If Israel were to keep all of that natural gas for itself, it would hold enough reserves to supply Israel's gas needs for 100 years. In the blink of an eye, Israel went from gas famine to gas feast.

According to the US Geological Survey's (USGS) Energy Resources Program, those reserves rival the largest known gas reserves in the world.

The USGS estimates the undiscovered oil and gas resources of the Levant Basin Province as being equivalent to 1.68 billion barrels of oil, and 122 trillion cubic feet (tcf) of gas. The entire eastern Mediterranean, the USGS estimates, could yield 345 tcf of gas and 3.4 billion barrels of oil.

The value of the Levant Basin's natural gas, according to experts, could be as much as $300 billion.

To put this in perspective, Russia's West Siberian Basin, the world's largest known gas basin, holds 643 tcf of gas, meaning this discovery could catapult Israel into an energy superpower rivaling Russia, the Middle East, and North Africa.

For Israel, whose energy supplies were severely threatened during the uprisings and conflicts in the Middle East known as the Arab Spring, the ability to supply all of its own energy needs and become a major world exporter would profoundly change the Jewish state's place in the world.

But Israel's claim to these new, rich energy sources is hardly going unchallenged.

These huge oil and gas reserves in the Mediterranean Sea are surrounded by Israel, Greece, Turkey, Cyprus, Syria, and Lebanon, and could one day create a new Persian Gulf. And just as the discovery of oil in the Persian Gulf made the region a major player in the Great Game, the Mediterranean version of the Persian Gulf, with its major hydrocarbon reserves, could change the geopolitical landscape in profound ways.

It could also become the epicenter of regional or even worldwide conflict.

♖

ISRAEL ISN'T THE only country that believes it holds the rights to this unprecedented energy discovery. As soon as the discovery was announced, neighboring Lebanon triggered a new geopolitical conflict by claiming a portion of the gas field lay in Lebanese territorial waters in Lebanon's Exclusive Economic Zone (EEZ).

To bolster its claim, the company delivered maps to the UN—claims Israel promptly dismissed. Technically, the two countries have been at war for years, though there have been sporadic ceasefires and attempts at peace negotiations.

Further complicating the issue is the 1982 UN Convention on Law of the Sea, which divides the world's subsea mineral rights.

Israel, like the U.S., has never ratified that agreement. The Lebanese Hezbollah, an organization that has repeatedly stated it does not recognize the legitimacy of the State of Israel, continues to dispute the ownership of the Levant Basin.

The Levant Basin

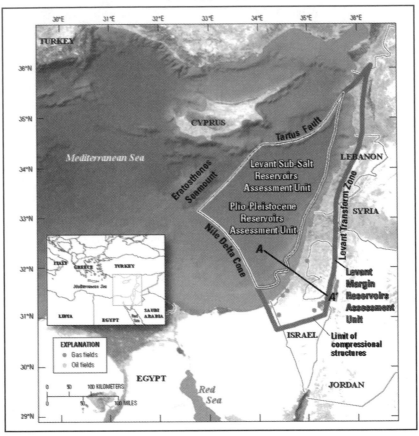

While much of the world has, so far, remained on the sidelines as interested spectators, the U.S. has wasted no time in adding metaphorical fuel to the fire. Turning its back on its long-time Middle East ally, the Obama Administration endorsed the Lebanese claim.

At the same time, Israel signed a bilateral energy development agreement with Cyprus. Turkey announced an offshore drilling deal with Shell Oil nearby and announced that the Israeli-Cypriot energy exploration deal was illegal. Meanwhile, both Russia and the U.S. have beefed up their military presence in the area.

Further complicating the picture, much of the known gas reserves, due to their depth and location, pose significant difficulties in extraction and transportation.

Much of the potential natural gas lies in waters up to 6,500 feet deep. Some of the countries disputing ownership of the Levant Basin, such as Greece, may not have the assets or expertise to develop a portion of the basin on their own, and would have to find an American, Russian, Arab, or other energy company as a development partner and ally.

The other wild card in this section of the Great Game is transportation of liquefied natural gas (LNG).

Currently, Israel can easily supply LNG to its neighbors in Egypt, Gaza, the West Bank, and Jordan. But to send its gas farther, Israel would have to choose one of four options, each with its own geopolitical consequences.

- Export gas via a planned LNG export terminal at Vassiliko, Cyprus, and then ship gas to Europe or, via the Red Sea to China and the rest of Asia.
- Build a natural gas pipeline under the Mediterranean Sea to Turkey to reach European markets.
- Build an overland pipeline to Turkey.
- Construct a $5 billion one-train floating offshore LNG export terminal in Israeli waters.

Currently, Israel has a memorandum of understanding with Cyprus and an agreement with Gazprom, the giant Russian energy company that includes various transport options. Tensions have been high between Turkey and Cyprus since the Turkish invasion and occupation of northern Cyprus in 1974.

Turkish experts also point out that a pipeline from Israel to Turkey's Ceyhan port is a quarter of that to the Greek mainland, though there has been animosity between Israel and Turkey since Israeli naval forces boarded a Turkish ship carrying aid to the Gaza Strip in 2010, killing eight Turkish activists and an American-Turkish citizen. Apologies were made, but tensions linger.

Israel also has several ongoing territorial disagreements in the area. A maritime boundary dispute between Israel and Lebanon could limit development in prospective regions of the eastern Mediterranean, since over 300 square miles in the Levant Basin remain disputed by both sides.

Add in the power of the Organization of the Petroleum Exporting

Countries (OPEC), and it would be difficult to imagine a more volatile series of scenarios.

But there's still one more complication: in 2013, Israel—still one of our staunchest allies—took $5.5 billion in emergency measures to save the U.S. dollar from collapsing against the Israeli shekel.

Though little reported at the time, the maneuver by the Bank of Israel had profound effects, not only in the value of the U.S. dollar, but the value of the Euro as well.

Would Israel take such measures again in the wake of weakening U.S. support for Israel's energy future?

That would be just one of the many questions with major implications in the Great Game.

17

The Endgame

In 1839, a young English intelligence officer by the name of Arthur Conolly coined the phrase "The Great Game." Sixty-one years later, it was immortalized in Rudyard Kipling's famous novel Kim.

Each knew the Great Game quite well. Conolly actually lived it . . . until 1842. At the age of 34, the Game cost him his life in northern India. Kipling spun tales about it, and by the time of his own death in 1936, he had won the Nobel Prize for Literature as the greatest British writer of his time.

As it happens, both of these men have personal meaning to me. I share a professional kinship with Conolly, having first been an intelligence officer (a "game" in its own right), before spending the bulk of my life in energy and university teaching. Meanwhile, Kipling has long been one of my inspirations, with *Kim* being my favorite adventure story.

Both used "The Great Game" to describe the competition between two empires—British and Russian—to control Central Asia. Then, the methods of control were political and military.

But as you have witnessed in this book, the *new* Great Game involves many more players. And this time, it revolves around more than just the control of any particular region.

The phrase may have begun as a way to explain the 19th century contest over places like India, Afghanistan and the Hindu Kush. These days, however, there is no part of the world escaping its influence.

What started with the movement of armies now translates into the survival of markets, commerce, industry, economies . . . of life itself. This very serious—and occasionally, very deadly game—is waged on an ever-changing chessboard of interests and trade.

Yet there is one common denominator, one continuing thread running throughout the entire modern version of this very old game.

Energy.

Nations do not always go to war only over the sources, trade routes, and distribution of energy. But energy is never very far from their minds. You can't fight a war or "live the peace" afterward without it.

In this rapidly changing global landscape, access to energy underpins national purpose, firms up one people's regard for another, animates ideas of security and defense, and provides justification for what is done and threatened.

It also, in large measure, determines who among the seven *billion* human beings living on our planet today will be still walking on it tomorrow.

As these pages have revealed, this is a serious business. And the competitions over energy—both raw materials and the technology necessary for its use—are becoming more intense and sinister.

These are not exceptions to normal life. Regrettably, they have become an enduring part of it. Our recognition of that reality is long overdue.

However, one aspect of this "new normal" continues to escape notice. Energy has been categorized (in my view, quite incorrectly) as simply a contest itself.

The objective here, if the pundits and other talking heads are to be believed, is to find what will save us from an addiction to oil. Yet this is not, and never will be, the real issue.

Looking for a "silver bullet" has occasioned the spotlight being placed on natural gas, coal (traditional, liquefied, synthetic), biofuels (ethanol, algae, biological waste products), nuclear (both fission and fusion), solar, wind, geothermal, even wave and tidal power. For each, there are adherents claiming this energy source will save us from oil.

Well, here's the reality: Our future will be found in an integrated energy *balance*. There will be a greater number of different types of sources, each having a range of applications. Our dependence will rest on the *totality* of that balance, not on some winner-take-all approach.

Our key here—and the next demanded stage in advancement—involves making separate energy sources interchangeable. In the process, the more efficient networking and usage of energy is essential.

This next massive adventure is not without its risks. After all, having more access points for more energy types can simply increase the pieces on the chessboard of conflict (and an extension of The Great Game into new and unsavory manifestations).

But it also provides an exciting prospect, a chance to do what I like doing best . . . pushing the envelope. Readily available and low-cost energy is the single biggest positive step in reversing human misery worldwide.

Take one simple example. The leading cause of death in the least advantaged regions is the lack of clean water. The single most essential ingredient in providing potable water is the energy to run local water treatment facilities, preferably those at the village level.

Figure out how to integrate the new energy grid on a global scale and we save lives. Lots of them.

Every risk also provides a reverse—an opportunity that was not there beforehand. While we keep one eye on the continuing global tensions, let's keep the other on what the energy revolution can accomplish for average folks living average lives.

Perhaps J. Paul Getty was right about who was winning and losing in the traditional energy battle. The meek inherit the earth, he suggests, but it is the strong that control what runs it.

On the other hand, the pivotal point at which we find ourselves today may provide a possible alternative.

We may not win this one either. The forces that have determined The Great Game for centuries are showing no signs of letting up.

Yet that also reminds me of what one of my heroes proclaimed almost 72 years ago, "This is not the end. This is not even the beginning of the end. But it is, perhaps, the end of the beginning."

Winston Churchill said this in November of 1942, after word arrived of a victory over Rommel at El Alamein in the "Battle of Egypt." This first real victory after a string of stinging defeats would rally the Allies during a very bloody version of The Great Game.

Something called World War II.

The Great Game

ABOUT THE AUTHOR

Dr. Kent Moors

KENT IS AN INTERNATIONALLY RECOGNIZED expert in oil and natural gas policy, risk management, emerging market economic development, and market risk assessment.

He serves as an advisor to the highest levels of the U.S., Russian, Kazakh, Bahamian, Iraqi, and Kurdish governments, to the governors of several U.S. states, and to the premiers of two Canadian provinces. He's served as a consultant to private companies, financial institutions and law firms in 25 countries, and has appeared more than 1,400 times as a featured radio-and-television commentator. He appears regularly on ABC, BBC, Bloomberg TV, CBS, CNN, NBC, Russian RTV, CCTV China and the Fox Business Network.

Kent is also a former professor in the Graduate Center for Social and Public Policy at Duquesne University, where he directed the Energy Policy Research Group.

A prolific writer and lecturer, his six books, more than 750 professional and market publications, and over 250 private/public sector presentations and workshops have appeared in 44 countries.

Kent delivers the latest energy news from his travels around the world in his role as a consultant for major companies and governments in his free newsletter *Oil & Energy Investor*.

It's available at: www.oilandenergyinvestor.com

MONEY MAP PRESS: YOUR MAP TO FINANCIAL FREEDOM

THE BIGGEST CHALLENGE FACING investors today is an almost complete lack of confidence.

But the solution is not to abandon the world of investing. Rather it's recognizing that it's a completely different world—with a different set of rules.

Play by the old rules, and you lose. Understand the new rules . . . and you can win the game.

That's what *Money Map Press* is all about.

Led by a team of expert investment strategists—with decades of experience between them—we uncover global trends well before the mainstream media takes notice.

So whether you're just starting out or planning your retirement, *Money Map Press* gives you actionable information you need to enjoy financial independence. It's what we do.

Here's to securing your financial freedom in the new global economy.

Good Investing,
Mike Ward
Publisher

MONEY MAP PRESS

Contact:
Money Map Press
16 West Madison Street
Baltimore, MD, 21201
Toll-free: 888.384.8339
International: +1.410.226.2069
Fax: 1.410.622.3050
Website: http://moneymappress.com